Producer & Editor: **Dalit Nemirovsky**
Production assistant: **Moria Goldstein**
Producer & Advisor: **Mati Broudo**

Researcher/Writer: **Lisa Goldman**
Introduction: **Gal Uchovsky**
Proofreading: **Melinda Bánki**

Photography: **Natan Dvir**
Graphic design: **Lahav Halevy, BigEyes Design**
Maps: **Dan Gershony**
Printed in Israel by: **A.R. Printing**

Although every effort has been made to ensure that the information in this book is as up to date and as accurate as possible at the time of going to press, some details are liable to change.

Israeli library cataloguing in publication data.
A catalogue record of this book is available from the Israeli Library.

ISBN 978-965-90997-3-3

Additional Photography:
p. 49 second right photo and middle left photo - courtesy of Sushi Samba; p. 50 bottom left photo - courtesy of Eretz Israel Museum Shop; p. 82 top left photo-courtesy of Arbitman's; p. 156 bottom left photo, p. 157 top photo - courtesy of Kastiel; p. 170 top right photo - courtesy of Manta Ray; p. 193 top photo- courtesy of Design by Riva; p. 192 top left photo and bottom right photo by Adi Segal/Blue Press; p. 195 top photo courtsey of Jaffa Port.

Contact:
Crossfields TLV
POB 14029, Tel Aviv 61140, Israel
info@cftlv.com
www.cityguidetelaviv.com

City Guide **Tel Aviv**

Contents

I am delighted to introduce the second edition of City Guide Tel Aviv, which has been published to coincide with Tel Aviv's centennial celebrations. With this edition we aim to bring to our readers and Tel Aviv's visitors a more extensive overview of the city's offering, and to present Tel Aviv for what it is in our eyes – a dynamic, hedonistic, multi-cultural Mediterranean metropolis that can easily compete with any major European city in terms of culture, fashion, culinary offerings, nightlife and leisure activities.

Tel Aviv is rapidly gaining international recognition for its hip nightlife, exciting gastronomic culture and Bauhaus-influenced architecture. Widely referred to as a living museum of Bauhaus architecture, Tel Aviv has been designated a World Cultural Heritage Site by UNESCO. Our goal in creating this guide is to present this unique Levantine metropolis to visitors from all over the globe. We have put together in one book the best places to eat, drink, shop, sleep and explore the city in order for the visitors to enjoy Tel Aviv the way we enjoy it. All the texts, photography and design were commissioned especially for this new edition.

How to use City Guide **Tel Aviv**

We have divided Tel Aviv into five distinct areas – the North End, City Center, the Heart of the City, the South End and Jaffa. Each chapter begins with an introduction that covers the area's history, characteristics and major landmarks. Following the introduction you will find detailed listings and descriptions of the area's most notable eating, entertainment, nightlife, shopping, hotels and culture options. Each location has a map number by its side that is marked on the area map featured at the beginning of each chapter. Additional recommendations are listed at the end of each chapter. City Guide Tel Aviv also includes an index, helpful tips for the visitor and comprehensive information about the centennial celebrations. I hope this book will guide you well to this 100 year-old city that is more vibrant, and has more culture and entertainment to offer than any other city I know.

Regards,

Dalit Nemirovsky, Editor

The Secret of Tel Aviv's Charm

Gal Uchovsky

Take London, for example. Day after day, millions of tourists shuffle along Oxford Street. Only a few turn off to South Molton Street, where the really interesting boutiques are located. The center of London, like the center of Paris or New York, is a combination of tourist sites and local secrets.

A big city always presents a challenge. If it's a really huge, famous city it has two levels – the one that's readily apparent to the eye, and the one that's hidden beneath the surface. Even Venice, which is one big tourist trap, has restaurants that specialize in food for locals only. Some of those restaurants have separate rooms for tourists - just in case some foreigners happen to wander in, disturbing the locals' peace and quiet. In fact, the more touristy a city is, the more likely the locals are to cluster in little buffer zones – or oases, if you will - to keep the colorful masses at bay and allow them to circumvent the masses of shuffling tourists.

Tel Aviv is not Amsterdam. For years it has been practically untouched by tourism. The standard Holy Land tour focuses, naturally, on Jerusalem, the Sea of Galilee, the Dead Sea and all the other places that have earned a stamp of quality indicating at least 5,000 years of history. Only recently has the world begun to discover Tel Aviv as some sort of Levantine version of Barcelona or Lisbon; and Tel Avivians are still at the stage of liking people who speak foreign languages – especially if they look cool.

It's not that Tel Aviv doesn't hide its insiders' secrets. It's just that the Israeli game of hide 'n seek is played between local, authentic urbanites and local suburbanites – those same two million people who live in the surrounding towns, for whom Tel Aviv is a place they visit for entertainment. Since suburbanites speak Hebrew, the codes that have been developed in order to avoid them are very sophisticated. You need a good eye and a lot of focus in order to discover the real Tel Aviv.

Because Tel Aviv's principal strength is its residents. I would not recommend that you visit Tel Aviv for the shopping - even though a discerning shopper will certainly find things to take home. I would not recommend that you visit for the food, even though the best hummus in the world is in Jaffa, at Ali Karavan, a small place that is open only until noon, where you share a table with construction workers and the waiters shoo you out the door as soon as you've swallowed your last bite. I would not recommend that you come for the architecture, either, even though we are very proud of the fact that Tel Aviv contains the highest concentration of Bauhaus buildings in the world.

There is actually only one thing that Tel Aviv is better at than anyplace else. As strange as this may sound, it's the coffee. Israel's greatest cultural achievement over the last decade has been the breaking of the secret code for perfect cappuccino preparation. Every Tel Aviv café – whether it's a shiny branch of a commercial chain or a casual neighborhood spot - serves excellent espresso at the right temperature. If it's not hot enough, you can return it and ask them to make you another. In fact, the only place in Tel Aviv that has bad coffee is McDonald's. We are grateful that there are few branches of McDonald's in Tel Aviv, and that children compose the majority of customers.

So why should you come to Tel Aviv? For the complete experience – the Mediterranean experience. To sit at the right spot on the beach, facing the sea, during those hours between late afternoon and sunset, and sip the right margarita. To stroll along Rothschild Boulevard at a certain hour of the afternoon, stopping at the right place for the perfect sandwich. To enjoy the insanely packed clubs and bars at night. In general, Tel Aviv is the kind of city that becomes much more charming after nightfall; during the small hours before sunrise, the city drinks and dances feverishly, and at full volume.

The daylight hours are a bit more complicated. Israelis don't like to discuss this subject, but the truth is that Tel Aviv is a bit reminiscent of the Third World. It is not a clean city. And some areas are full of service providers who get a kick out of cheating the tourists a bit. They don't want to mug you – they're not interested in stealing your suitcase, for example; they will just overcharge you a little. At the same time, in the more salubrious areas, salesclerks and business owners will spend an hour offering the tourist insider's tips on what to see and do, and where to stay and eat. And then there's the weather. Which is quite pleasant, relatively speaking, although the summer months are completely unbearable during most daylight hours. Which is why they invented air conditioners.

Confused? Don't worry. This is only the beginning. Because the Mediterranean air and the political situation have made Israelis seem a bit aggressive – particularly to a western tourist. With a handful of exceptions, the restaurants and bars that line the beachfront are full of tourist stalkers. They whistle at the babes in bikinis and make suggestive comments, and sometimes they even try to send them to some great shop that is owned by their uncle. Their only redeeming characteristic is that they are almost never violent. "No" is definitely a word they understand.

It's not coincidence that tourists used to pass up Tel Aviv. There are no big monuments – only small and trifling ones. Rothschild Boulevard, with its restored Bauhaus buildings, might be the only street in the city that is truly worth strolling. And even here you will be much better off knowing the territory: the length of the boulevard is lined with a mix of the trendiest hangouts and restaurants in the city, interspersed randomly with a few bars and restaurants that host God knows what kind of people.

Tel Aviv is a relatively small city, with large sections that are mostly residential. In order to be seduced and charmed by Tel Aviv's magic you need to use your legs and walk, and hope that it's not too hot. At any rate, take comfort in knowing that even the smallest kiosk is air-conditioned these days.

The real Tel Aviv stretches from the Yarkon in the north, to Jaffa in the south. Taken as a whole, it is a small patch of land that combines yesterday and tomorrow in a way that stirs the heart. It's a cliché to use expressions like "yesterday and tomorrow," but there is no other way to create a connection between the ultra-modern restaurant wrapped in plate-glass windows at the top of the Azrieli Center - from where you can see practically the entire country, from Ashkelon to Haifa and as far east as the Jerusalem hills – and the flea market in Jaffa, where time has stood still for many decades.

This is a city of falafel and sushi. The first one must be consumed while standing, remembering that there is always a hole in the bottom of the pita, through which the tehina dribbles down your shirt; the latter is served in a restaurant that is frequently overpriced, particularly given the quality of the Mediterranean fish that the proprietors use. And in order to make things simpler, getting dressed to go out in Tel Aviv is the easiest thing in the world – whether you're going jogging or to the opera (if you must). The essential garment is the cotton-knit T-shirt. If it is printed with an interesting graphic, you might even be rewarded with a few compliments.

There are very few occasions that necessitate the wearing of a suit in Tel Aviv – particularly when it's hot, which is most of the year, it is preferable to wear as little as possible. Tel Aviv is a casual city. There is no need for codes of conduct. Everything is open, right out on the table: just start chatting with your waiter, and pretty soon he'll ask where you are from, and how much you earn in a year.

So what is the ultimate Tel Aviv experience? What is the one thing you must do, otherwise your visit will have been pointless? There is no right answer to that question. Perhaps because there is no such thing as the one, ultimate Tel Aviv experience. Tel Aviv is a city that goes with the flow. Each morning, it decides anew what is interesting, what is annoying and where we are going. Perhaps the only way to conquer the city is simply to come over - to settle in and let it pull you into its gentle flow. Something will definitely happen. Something always happens in Tel Aviv. And with a little luck, it will happen to you.

Gal Uchovsky
Mazeh Street, Tel Aviv
May 2008

Gal Uchovsky is a film producer and screenwriter whose work includes international hits such as "Walk on Water" and "The Bubble", both directed by Eytan Fox. A veteran journalist and music critic, Uchovsky is also one of the judges on Israel's version of American Idol.

HOTEL CINEMA

Introduction

Lisa Goldman

Tel Aviv tends to surprise first-time visitors. They come expecting to find a provincial Middle Eastern city of plodding camels, ancient monuments, Oriental fantasies and armed combatants; instead, they discover a stylish, utterly contemporary Mediterranean metropolis filled with chic cafés, an exciting culture scene, fashionable boutiques, barely-clad beautiful people and a roaring nightlife.

For years, Tel Aviv was the jealously guarded secret of hip travelers – an alternative vacation destination that was edgier and more vibrant than the overpriced, touristy cities that dot the Mediterranean basin. Only very recently have international travel writers recognized the city's many attributes - notably, of course, the clubs, restaurants and art galleries.

But the real source of Tel Aviv's seductive powers is something less tangible. It is its overwhelming love of life. You see it in the uninhibited dancing on the bars; in the ever-crowded cafés, buzzing with laughter and conversation from morning until night; in the 24-hour holiday atmosphere during the long summer months; and in the furious creativity poured into the local theater, music and fashion scenes. There are very few cities that feel as strongly alive, self-confident and hedonistic – or that live so firmly in the present. And because Tel Aviv is relaxed, welcoming and homelike, the initial seduction usually evolves into a lifelong love affair.

Tel Aviv celebrates its 100th birthday this year. A famous photograph taken in 1909 shows a group of Zionist pioneers gathered on a beach near Jaffa, when it was still an outpost of the Ottoman Empire, dividing up a plot of land they named Ahuzat Bayit. Later, the fledgling settlement was renamed Tel Aviv, or Hill of Spring, after the Hebrew title of *Altneuland*, Theodore Herzl's seminal tract on modern Zionism.

From 1909-1932, Tel Aviv was a sleepy little village that developed slowly, in fits and stops. The predominant architectural style was eclectic – a mixture of Levantine, Central European and Oriental influences – and the street planning somewhat haphazard. At the beginning of the 1920s, two major events occurred and determined the city's future: Jaffa's commercial center moved to

Tel Aviv, following violent confrontations between the Jewish and Arab communities of that ancient port city; and Sir Patrick Geddes created a modern urban plan for Tel Aviv, based on the Garden City concept.

Geddes was a visionary who planned the city so that it would answer its residents' spiritual and material needs, by taking into account factors ranging from climate and social structure to income. He believed in fostering human interaction by bringing people together naturally in public places, such as squares, parks and streets; he did not believe in separating the commercial center from the residential areas, lest the former become ghost towns during non-working hours. Residential buildings were to be low-rise, airy, aesthetically pleasing and inexpensive.

Starting from 1932, a third historical event proved to be the decisive factor in creating a permanent, definitive stamp on Tel Aviv's character and appearance. The rise of Hitler brought a massive influx of German-Jewish refugees to the tiny city. The architects who designed the residential buildings for those refuges were trained in the Bauhaus style – which, with its merging of art and functionality, was uniquely suited to Geddes's vision. Tel Aviv was their blank canvas: within two decades, an estimated 5,000 buildings in the Bauhaus-influenced International, or Modern, style of clean lines, curved balconies and geometric shapes were constructed all over Tel Aviv and Jaffa. Thus was born the first – and only – Bauhaus city.

Fifty years later, UNESCO designated the White City – so called for the brilliance of its original whitewashed buildings – a World Heritage Site. Once the most modern city in the world, Tel Aviv is now frequently – and perhaps ironically – referred to as a "living museum" of Modern architecture. Most of those Bauhaus buildings have been terribly neglected, but they are being restored at an ever-increasing pace to reflect the city's newfound pride in its heritage.

Nearly one century after Patrick Geddes submitted his plan for Tel Aviv to the city's first mayor, Meir Dizengoff, his basic vision of a liveable urban space has held: Tel Aviv suffers from common urban problems like traffic jams and pollution, but it remains a social city that is lined with tree shaded boulevards and dotted with green parks and squares where people gather at all hours of the day and night. There is clearly an ongoing struggle between Geddes' plan

and the needs of a 21st century metropolis, but so far the balance between preservation and modernization has held.

The anchor for all this modernity is Jaffa, which is frequently called the oldest functioning port city in the world. Today, the two cities are officially one – called Tel Aviv-Jaffa – but they look and feel very different. Jaffa is awash in ancient historical monuments and redolent of the Middle East, while Tel Aviv is almost devoid of monuments and feels more Levantine than Middle Eastern. In many ways, though, they complement and complete one another.

A stroll or bicycle ride from Jaffa to the Yarkon Park in the north is really a journey through Tel Aviv's short, but fascinating, history. Start at the ancient port, where the first modern Zionist pioneers disembarked at the end of the nineteenth century; continue on to Neve Tzedek, where Aharon Chelouche, scion of a prominent Jaffa family, purchased a plot of land and established the first Jewish neighborhood outside of Jaffa in the early 1880s; next are the neighborhoods of southern and central Tel Aviv, where the Bauhaus influence of the 1930s and 1940s predominates; and, finally, you will come to the boxy, charmless structures that were built during the 1950s and 1960s, when Israel was a new state with urgent housing needs and little money. Along the way you will see the grand experiments of the 1970s – like the Dizengoff Center, which was a success, and the raised pedestrian bridge over Dizengoff Circle, which was not. Interspersed between these 20-year stages of Tel Aviv's evolution - as witnessed by its architecture - you will see bland contemporary high-rise office buildings and new luxury apartment buildings that attest to the city's continued surge forward, as it consolidates its position as a major international commerce and culture capital.

One of the Tel Aviv's great, simple pleasure is a leisurely stroll or bicycle ride up and down the beachfront promenade, along the Mediterranean coast, from ancient Jaffa to the green expanses of Hayarkon Park in the north. On Saturday afternoons the promenade is packed with strolling couples and families, street artists, hucksters and musicians. It is a major gathering place and a center of this Mediterranean city's life.

In general, the joy of Tel Aviv is found in its simple pleasures. There is the café culture, for example: it is almost impossible to walk for more than 50 meters anywhere in the city without coming across a café. Tel Avivians gather at cafés to read the morning newspapers with their coffee, to work on their laptops (free wireless Internet connections are the norm), to hold business meetings, to gossip with friends. For a visitor who wants to soak up the local culture, a café is the ideal place to start – and linger, for hours at a time.

For those who have experienced it, there is nothing quite like Tel Aviv's nightlife. It is anarchistic, cutting edge and hedonistic, but neither threatening nor intimidating. All the negative factors that characterize nightlife in London and New York – the aggressive posing, the hostile bouncers, the pushy drunkards – are completely absent in Tel Aviv. Everything starts very late, with bars opening after 10 p.m. and clubs after midnight. In some parts of the city, 4 o'clock on a Saturday morning feels like rush hour.

Tel Aviv has plenty of serious culture, too. There are dozens of art galleries, a critically acclaimed opera company and a world-renowned symphony orchestra, conducted by Zubin Mehta. There are around twelve theaters, from Habimah, Israel's national theater, to fringe theater; per capita, Tel Aviv has one of the highest numbers of theater attendees in the world. Some, like the Gesher Theater and Do Touch, offer performances with surtitles in English.

All over the city, on any given night, there are poetry readings, gallery exhibition openings, experimental theater performances, live avant-garde jazz by local and international artists, and performances of local pop, rock, Indy and folk music. The city draws up-and-coming artists from all over the world, and it buzzes with creative energy.

Social attitudes are remarkably open in Tel Aviv, by any standards. Frequently included in the top ten gay-friendly cities in the world, it hosts a hugely popular annual gay pride parade but has few gay clubs and bars, for the simple reason that there is no ghettoization of gays and straights in Tel Aviv.

The sun shines on most days in Tel Aviv, but the summers are terribly hot and humid and the winters, while short, can be damp and chilly. The best time to come for a visit is in the spring – particularly in March, when the evenings are still cool enough to merit a light sweater and the days are warm enough for the beach. If you do come in July-August or September, the heat will make daytime touring nearly impossible – unless you have a fondness for tropical weather. Save your energy for the humid nights, with their all-night party atmosphere. And don't worry about walking around the city alone, late at night: violent urban crime is practically unheard of in Tel Aviv.

Here are some little things to know about getting along in the city:

- The local area code is (03). You don't need it if you are calling a number in Greater Tel Aviv, of course, and you must drop the zero if you are calling from abroad. The area code for Israel is 972.
- Taxi drivers tend to see tourists as soft targets. Remember, they are required by law to turn on their meter (called a "moh-neh" in Hebrew). It is not customary to tip taxi drivers.
- Restaurant wait staff, on the other hand, do expect a gratuity of about 15 percent. Tips are usually left in cash, even if you pay the bill with a credit card.
- Most businesses close on Friday afternoon, re-opening on Sunday morning. Cafés and restaurants tend to stay open for the weekend, although there are many exceptions so it is always wise to check before going out. Clubs, pubs, kiosks, cinemas and theatres are all open.
- Whatever happens, you never need to worry about eating well in Tel Aviv. Even the simplest cafés serve delicious fresh salads and sandwiches for reasonable prices. And, of course, the coffee is always good.
- In Tel Aviv, "dressed up" means upscale casual. You can leave the suits at home, although trendy and fashionable is just as important here as it is in any major city.

Don't worry if we locals don't smile at you very often. We're not being cold – just cool, in the fashionable sense. And we warm up quickly.

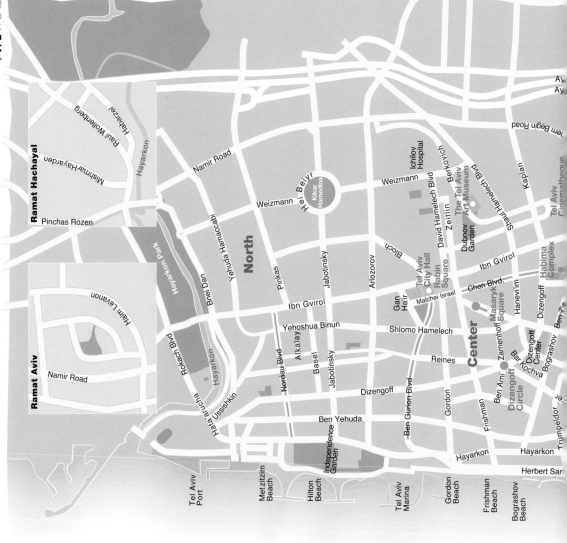

Ramat Hachayal
Habarzel
Raul Wollenberg
Mishmar Hayarden
Hayarkon
Pinchas Rozen

Ramat Aviv
Haim Levanon
Namir Road

Namir Road
Weizmann
Hei Beiyr
Kikar Hamedina
Weizmann
Ichilov Hospital
Berkovich
The Tel Aviv Art Museum
Shaul Hamelech Blvd
Kaplan
Tel Aviv Cinematheque
Menachem Begin Road
Hayarkon Park
Bnei Dan
Yehuda Hamaccabi
North
Pinkas
Jabotinsky
Arlozorov
Bloch
David Hamelech Blvd
Zeitlin
Dubnov Garden
Tel Aviv City Hall
Rabin Square
Ibn Gvirol
Habima Complex
Chen Blvd.
Malchei Israel
Gan Ha'ir
Ibn Gvirol
Masaryk Square
Hanevi'im
Dizengoff
Yehoshua Binun
Shlomo Hamelech
Center
Rokach Blvd
Alkalay
Nordau Blvd
Basel
Jabotinsky
Reines
Zamenhoff
Dizengoff Center
Bograshov
Bar Kochva
Hayarkon
Hata'arucha
Ussishkin
Dizengoff
Ben Ami
Dizengoff Circle
Ben Gurion Blvd
Gordon
Frishman
Ben Yehuda
Independence Garden
Trumpeldor
Hayarkon
Hayarkon
Herbert Sam
Tel Aviv Port
Metzitzim Beach
Hilton Beach
Tel Aviv Marina
Gordon Beach
Frishman Beach
Bograshov Beach

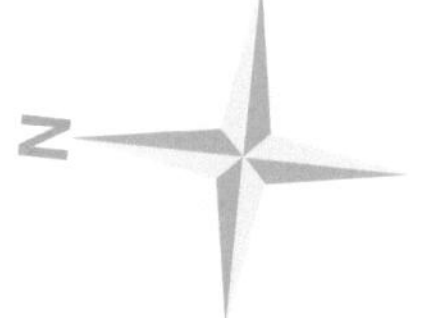

Kerem Hateimanim
Sheinkin
Heart
Halevi
Lincoln
Menachem B
Banana Beach
Hayarkon
Tha Carmel Market
Balfour
Albert Square
Mazeh
Shefer
Nachalat Binyamin
Allenby
Montefiore
Bezalel Yafe
Nachmani
The Dolphinarium
Hamasger
Rival
Yad Harutzim
Harakevet
Hatzfira
Shalom Tower
Yavne
Shadal
Barzilay
Gan Hachashmal
Koifman
Neve Zedek
Lilienblum
Levontin
hachashmal
Heichal Hatalmud
Neve Sha'anan
Derech Yafo
Shabazi
Chelouche
Yechieli
South
Levinsky
Wolfson
Suzanne Dallal Center
Matalon
Herzl
Har Zion Blvd
Frenkel
Alma Beach
Eilat
Elifelet
Abarbanel
Vital
Florentin
Washington Blvd
Tirza
Nechama
American Colony
Salame
Kibutz Galuyot
Alfasi
Ben Yair
Yoezer
Noga
Old Jaffa
Hatzorfim
Flea Market
Yochanan
Hzchuchit
Hapninim
Olei Zion
The Port
Paster
Yehuda Margoza
Yehuda Hayamit
Ben Zvi
Jerusalem
Jaffa Port
Hadolphin
Yefet
Shivtei Israel
Jaffa
Kedem
Agami Area
Jerusalem Blvd
Toulouse
Yefet

North End

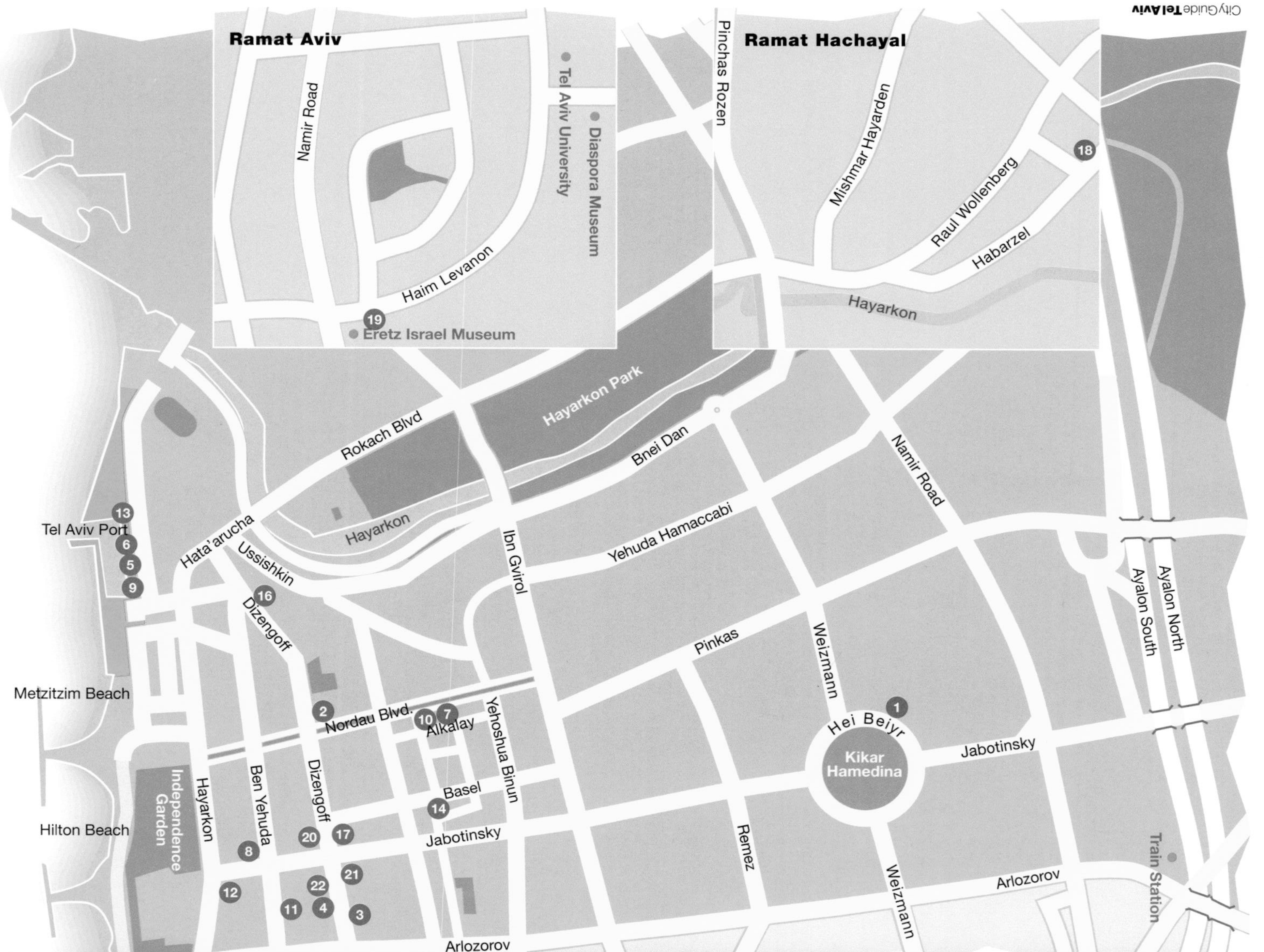

Ramat Aviv
Namir Road
Tel Aviv University
Diaspora Museum
Haim Levanon
19
Eretz Israel Museum
Pinchas Rozen
Ramat Hachayal
Mishmar Hayarden
18
Raul Wollenberg
Habarzel
Hayarkon
Hayarkon Park
Rokach Blvd
Bnei Dan
Namir Road
13
Tel Aviv Port
6
5
9
Hata'arucha
Hayarkon
Ussishkin
Ibn Gvirol
Yehuda Hamaccabi
Ayalon South
Ayalon North
16
Dizengoff
Pinkas
Weizmann
Metzitzim Beach
2
Nordau Blvd.
10
7
Alkalay
Yehoshua Binun
1
Hei Beiyr
Kikar Hamedina
Jabotinsky
Independence Garden
Hayarkon
Ben Yehuda
Dizengoff
Basel
14
Hilton Beach
20
17
Jabotinsky
Remez
8
21
12
22
11
4
3
Weizmann
Arlozorov
Train Station
Arlozorov

North End

The north end of Tel Aviv is solidly bourgeois and Ashkenazi and feels far more influenced by Europe than the Middle East. It is quiet, green, prosperous and pleasantly dull. This is where the icons of upper middle class Tel Aviv are located – like Kikar Hamedina, with its European designer shops, Assuta Hospital, which is private and caters to the wealthy, and the Herzliya Gymnasium, one of the country's most prestigious high schools.

This is possibly one of the last places in Israel where it is common to see elegantly dressed septuagenarian women, with bags that match their shoes, sitting in cafés and chatting in German or Hungarian – or in carefully enunciated, grammatically perfect, old-fashioned Hebrew. It is an aging neighborhood, although recently there has been an influx of young urban professionals who are looking for the closest thing to the suburbs within the big city. You can spot them easily: look for the thirtysomething couples – she with a perky blonde ponytail and he with a Montblanc pen in his shirt pocket – pushing a baby in a carriage and pulling a dog on a leash.

Despite its socio-economic prestige, this area is not architecturally distinguished. Unlike the rest of Tel Aviv, the north end is not strongly characterized by the Modernist look and there are few noteworthy examples of International style low-rise residential buildings. There are, however, many examples of utilitarian-looking residences that were constructed in the 1960s and 1970s – especially around Yehuda Hamaccabi. The most prominent aesthetic characteristic of this area is the high concentration of green parks – especially Hayarkon Park, the jewel in the crown.

The north end of Tel Aviv is also a major shopping area for upscale designer clothes. It has a high concentration of elegant – and expensive – boutiques, particularly on North Dizengoff and around Kikar Hamedina.

Hilton Beach and **Hof Metzitzim**

The two major beaches in the north end have provided lots of material for Israeli cultural references. Hilton Beach, named for the hotel above it, is known as the gay beach. That doesn't mean that heterosexuals are unwelcome – far from it – but there is a certain "check me out" vibe between the extremely well groomed men who frequent Hilton Beach.

Hof Metzitzim is Hebrew for "Peeping Toms' Beach." The name is derived from an Israeli cult film, made in the early 1970s, that starred major rock stars like Arik Einstein. The bohemian scene to which Einstein and his friends belonged centered on this beach. There was a lot of boy-girl action in the film – much of it considered quite risqué back then, when Israel was a much more conservative place.

North **Dizengoff, Basel** Square and **Kikar Hamedina**

When fashionable Israelis with disposable income – or a sizable overdraft – go shopping, they usually head to North Dizengoff, Basel Square and Kikar Hamedina. Each has clusters of exclusive boutiques, with the types of designers varying from one area to the next.

North Dizengoff is sometimes referred to as fashion row. This is where nearly all of Israel's most prominent homegrown designer boutiques are located. The local talent is quite impressive and often unique, ranging from elegant evening gowns to trendy club gear, with well-cut business suits and casual apparel a strong presence, as well. Several of the designers have won prestigious international fashion awards.

There are also many bridal boutiques in this area. On Thursday, the most popular day to marry, stiffly gowned and carefully coiffed young women emerge in the afternoons from the boutiques to be photographed and filmed, before they enter the waiting car that will whisk them off to the ceremony.

North Dizengoff is also a pleasant place to stroll, café hop and window shop. It is tree-and-bench lined and remarkably quiet in comparison with the southern stretch of the street.

The shops around Basel Square are not quite as cutting-edge as those on North Dizengoff. There are a few boutiques that specialize in fashionable, expensive maternity and baby clothes and some branches of well-known Israeli designer boutiques. Otherwise, this is really more of a place to purchase accessories – from scented candles to imported Italian dishes and locally designed jewelry – or to enjoy a leisurely afternoon at a fashionable café. The atmosphere at Basel Square is unmistakably laid back and prosperous.

And then there is Kikar Hamedina, the name that is synonymous with money – usually new, and in great quantities. This circular "square" has the highest concentration of prestigious international name brands in the city, from Rolex and Bulgari to Ralph Lauren and Versace; in many ways, it resembles a big duty free shop. And indeed, Kikar Hamedina is the place where Israeli plutocrats who don't have time to hop over to Europe for a weekend shopping spree come to purchase their clothes and jewelry. Interestingly, because of a municipal zoning law there is only one café on Kikar Hamedina; the rest are clustered on the side streets that are like spokes sticking out from a wheel.

Kikar Hamedina's expensive shops and elite reputation contrast rather oddly with its somewhat run down appearance. Air conditioner hoses drip into plastic bottles outside shops where couture dresses are sold. Display windows are sometimes smudged with finger prints, and building facades with flaking paint are common. The grassy, circular park is neglected and badly kept, too. But soon the park will disappear. It is privately owned and plans are underway to make it the site of a luxury-housing complex, after the owner won a 20-year battle with local residents and the municipality.

'he **North Port** ɩnd **Hayarkon** Park

For years, Tel Aviv's North Port was a site of major urban blight. Recently it underwent a refurbishing and gentrification process and is now one of the most popular areas in the city to eat, shop, stroll and troll the nightlife. There are parts that still look like a port, with the apparatus for unloading ships' cargo left intact – although it is no longer used – and the leisure areas are built around them. This was a conscious decision, and the result is an interesting juxtaposition of modern, fashionable Tel Aviv with its recent past.

The waterfront has a wooden boardwalk that is lined with cafés, restaurants and bars and the sections that are set back from the water are packed with some of the city's trendiest nightclubs. There is almost never a time when the port is empty of people. Joggers appear early in the morning, later on families and young couples come to stroll the boardwalk and stop for lunch at one of the pretty cafés. After dark the port becomes a major nightlife scene, with music spilling out the doors of the clubs and dance bars.

A stroll from the north port up to Hayarkon Park, Israel's largest public park, is a uniquely Tel Aviv experience, and highly recommended – especially on a lazy Saturday afternoon.

At nearly 4 kilometers square, Hayarkon Park rivals New York's Central Park in both size and beauty. The paths along the riverbank are one of the most popular places in the city for recreational bicycling. Families picnic on the tree-shaded grass and there are even regular cricket games between teams of ex-pat Indian diamond merchants and locals. Hayarkon Park is a great, multicultural Israeli gathering place – magically peaceful and pleasant.

The park features an aviary, a waterpark and an artificial lake. The whole area is well maintained by the municipality, and treated with an unusual degree of respect in a country where public spaces are often sadly abused.

Yehuda Hamaccabi St.

Yehuda Hamaccabi Street and the surrounding streets were planned and built during the 1960s, as was Tel Aviv University. Prior to that, the city ended at Hayarkon Park. Like the rest of the north end, this is a prestigious, upper class neighborhood. The tree-lined street is notable mostly for its cafés and the side streets for their quiet, very middle class atmosphere. There is not a lot to draw a visitor here, but it's a very pleasant place to stroll or stop for a coffee if you find yourself in the neighborhood.

This area really feels like a rather Germanic (some say it is reminiscent of Frankfurt), well-ordered suburb in the city. There are clusters of private homes with little gardens, for example – a sort of realization of the city's founders' vision of a "garden city."

North of the **Yarkon**: **Ramat Aviv,** and Tel Aviv **University**

Greater Tel Aviv branched northward during the 1960s, with the establishment of upscale suburbs such as Ramat Aviv Gimmel. As soon as one crosses the Yarkon and enters Haim Levanon Street, the change in atmosphere is obvious. The homes and apartment blocks are clearly suburban – well spaced and comfortable, but not architecturally distinguished.

Haim Levanon Street leads past museums and up into Ramat Aviv, where the

Tel Aviv University campus is located. The green campus is a pleasant place to stroll, and the Diaspora Museum, which tells the story of the Jewish Nation's 2,000 year exile from the Land of Israel, is worth a visit.

Ramat Hachayal

Ramat Hachayal is so modern that it almost looks like something out of a science fiction film. The sleek office towers were built at the height of the high-tech boom. Today some of the most important global high tech firms have research and development offices in Ramat Hachayal. There are several excellent restaurants here, many of which have become a magnet for the fashionable downtown Tel Aviv crowd. With its clean, contemporary lines, obvious prosperity and cosmopolitan atmosphere, Ramat Hachayal symbolizes Tel Aviv's forward-looking, worldly attitude.

SCHREIBER UNIVERSITY ART GALLERY

Design

Blue Bandana

52 Hei Beiyar St., Kikar Hamedina
Tel. (03) 602 1686

Located in north Tel Aviv's most exclusive shopping area, Blue Bandana sells beautiful, unique home accessories to people with excellent taste. This small, stylish shop stocks an eclectic collection of handpicked items from all over the globe, with many designed exclusively for Blue Bandana. The stock is constantly updated, making each visit – and yes, there will be more than one - a pleasant journey of discovery. Ceramic dishes painted in deep, bold, difficult-to-achieve colors are carefully stacked on industrial style metal shelves that line the otherwise minimalist white space. Items from Blue Bandana are regularly featured in the pages of the country's most prestigious newspapers and magazines, invariably with a gushing description of their aesthetic appeal. A visit to Blue Bandana is frequently the catalyst for an epiphany: Suddenly, you discover how many things you lack. And you understand that you really, really need them.

[Map 1]

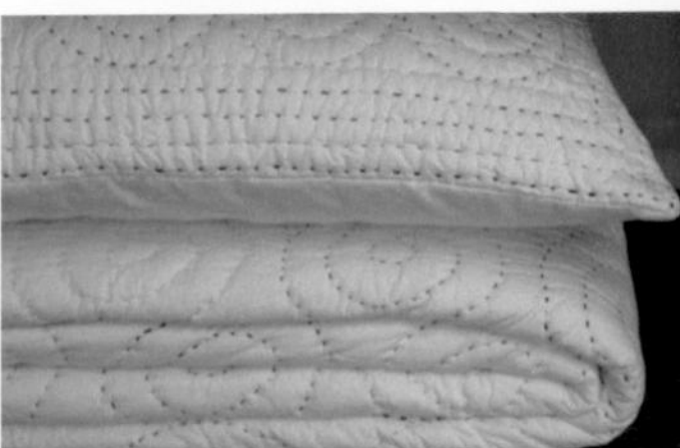

Fashion

[Map 2]

FabLab Fabiani

280 Dizengoff St.
Tel. (03) 602 5569
www.fablabfabiani.com

FabLab Fabiani focuses on innovative concepts, intelligence and integrity of design that advances fashion as an art form. Owner Diana Churges sees clothes as an expression of the wearer's emotions and their response to the world in which they exist – in other words, clothes as a means of expression, rather than escapism.

Her customers are intelligent women with strong personalities who seek avant garde, wearable fashion that expresses their personal vision. Ms. Churges travels widely to seek clothes, shoes and accessories by cutting edge designers whose works are unique and difficult to find, and which complement one another in order to form a cohesive collection at FabLab Fabiani.

[Map 3]

Fashion

Banot - Loulou Liam

212 Dizengoff St.
Tel. (03) 529 1175
www.loulouliam.com

Located in a renovated residential apartment, in a classic building on North Dizengoff Street, Banot is a striking combination of modern, urban sensibility and intimate, feminine awareness. The clean lines of the modern décor contrast with the evocative atmosphere of this three-room boutique to complement and reflect designer Loulou Liam's elegant seasonal collections. Loulou creates beautiful contemporary garments that are feminine, body conscious and sexy. Working with a primarily monochromatic color palette, with the occasional dash of color, she focuses on the silhouette, the fabric and the meticulous construction. Loulou's Second Skin lingerie collection is composed of sheer camisoles and underwear in breathable cotton with pontelle patterns, evoking a fresh, nostalgic look that completes the soft, feminine, sexy Banot look.

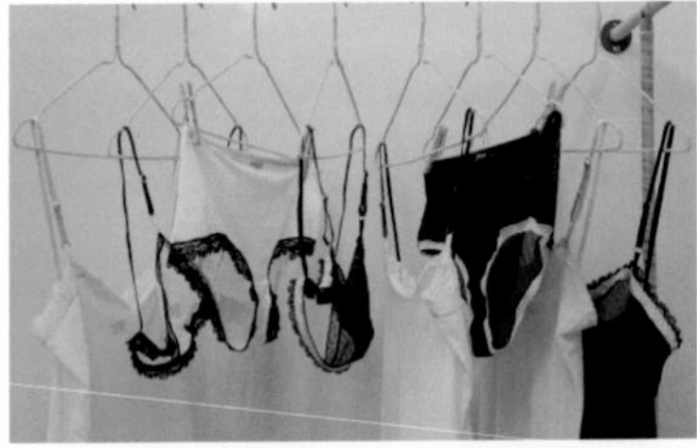

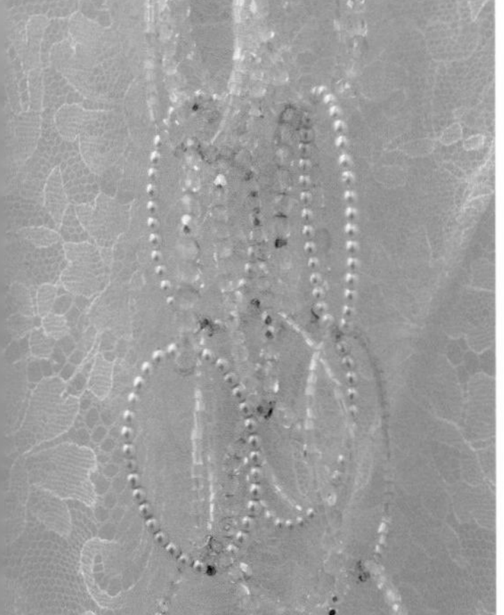

Fashion

Ossy Pri Hadash

209 Dizengoff St.
Tel. (03) 522 2768

[Map 4]

Upon entering Ossy Pri Hadash, one is transported to a world of classic, understated beauty and romance. The white-on-white décor of Ossy's tiny bridal boutique creates an island of minimalism, which highlights the designer's graceful gowns of soft silk, French lace and satin. Ossy's belief that a bride should be soft, gentle and pure is expressed in body-conscious styles made from the finest fabrics, cut to drape and move naturally. Each gown has beautiful details like hand-sewn beading or a woven ribbon back closure. The overall effect is slightly reminiscent of 1940s style, but indisputably modern. Ossy sews all the dresses by hand, in her studio nearby. "It's a lot of work," she says. "But I love it."

[Map 5]

Night, Café

Shalvata

3 Hata'arucha St. Tel Aviv port
Tel. (03) 544 1279

Named with tongue in cheek for one of Israel's biggest mental institutions, the sign over the entrance to this outdoor seaside bar/restaurant welcomes patrons to Shalvata, "the sanest place on earth." Shalvata also means "tranquility," which is very apt indeed. By day, this is a laid-back restaurant where patrons sprawl on the couches and lounge chairs that are shaded by palm frond umbrellas, enjoying simple, summer-appropriate meals like salads, sandwiches, pizzas and fried calamari. Shalvata is also a particularly lovely place to watch the sunset while enjoying a glass of chilled white wine.

At night, Shalvata becomes a breezy, friendly Mediterranean-resort style dance bar that attracts the beautiful and happy people with house-special frozen margaritas and excellent DJ's.

Night

Whisky a Go Go

3 Hata'arucha St., Tel Aviv port
Tel. (03) 544 0633
(054) 560 2262

Usually referred to by locals as "the whisky", Whisky a Go Go is one of Tel Aviv's hottest and best-known nightspots. This mega lounge bar's décor is rather striking: retro-chic chandeliers are suspended over the enormous wooden bar, there are red leather couches and flattering red-hued light that shows off the assets of the beautiful people to best effect. Altogether, the effect is intimate, warm and vaguely reminiscent of a nineteenth century New Orleans brothel. This is appropriate, given the sexy atmosphere at Whisky a Go Go – especially after midnight, when the excellent DJ's pump up the volume and the scene heats up. That's when the young and the beautiful start to dance around – and occasionally on - the crowded bar.

[Map 6]

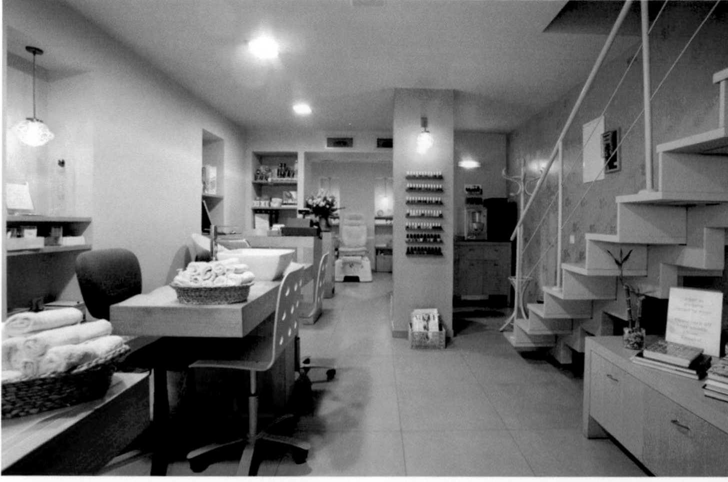

Beauty

Luck

5 Alkalay St., Basel Square
Tel. (03) 544 2252
www.luckworld.co.il

Luck provides a range of manicure, pedicure, foot massage and beauty treatments in a holistic, relaxing mini-spa environment. Every detail is tailored to maximize the nurturing, soothing atmosphere - from the request to turn mobile phones off, to the faultlessly professional staff. Whether you have stopped by for a quick, basic manicure, or whether you have put aside a few hours for a facial, Nirvana Foot Massage and Grace Manicure, you will leave feeling renewed and at peace. All Luck treatments can be purchased as a gift certificate for a loved one.

[Map 7]

Food

Benedict

171 Ben Yehuda St.
Tel. (03) 544 0345

[Map 8]

Benedict's ground-breaking concept is all about breakfast, all the time. This stylish-yet-intimate restaurant serves the best meal of the day, in all its glorious varieties and from the freshest ingredients, 24-hours a day, in surroundings that combine classic European style, contemporary New York chic and laid-back Israeli cool. It's a genius of an idea that encapsulates upscale comfort food, leisure and the best of Tel Aviv's lifestyle in one package. Benedict's breakfasts range from the English sausage-and-beans style to the lighter Mediterranean variety, but there is one constant: everything is delicious, and made from impeccably high-quality ingredients. Even the bread is baked on the premises, emitting a primordial smell that will bring smiles to the faces of both early morning risers and late-night revelers.

Bayit BaNamal, comme il faut house at the port

Hangar 26, Tel Aviv port
Tel. (03) 544 9211
www.comme-il-faut.com

[Map 9]

Founded by veteran fashion house comme il faut, Bayit BaNamal is a light, airy and architecturally distinguished modern space that brings fashion, culture, recreation and dining together under one roof. It includes fashion boutiques, shoe and jewelry shops, a spa for women, and a restaurant with a superb waterfront setting. The complex is open every day, including Saturday.

The comme il faut fashion house is renowned for its high quality, comfortable garments that are contemporary and timeless. The philosophy of the all-female design team is "fashion for real women."

The Coola spa caters exclusively to women, offering holistic face and body treatments. The spa also hosts a variety of workshops including belly dancing and yoga.

Located on the wooden boardwalk, with a beautiful view of the sea, the comme il faut café serves delicious, healthy-gourmet cuisine.

Every three months, Bayit BaNamal hosts a new exhibition of works by talented local artists and photographers, focusing primarily on feminist issues.

Shoes, Bags

Gaya

5 Alkalay St., Basel Square
Tel. (03) 602 2747
www.gayashoe.co.il

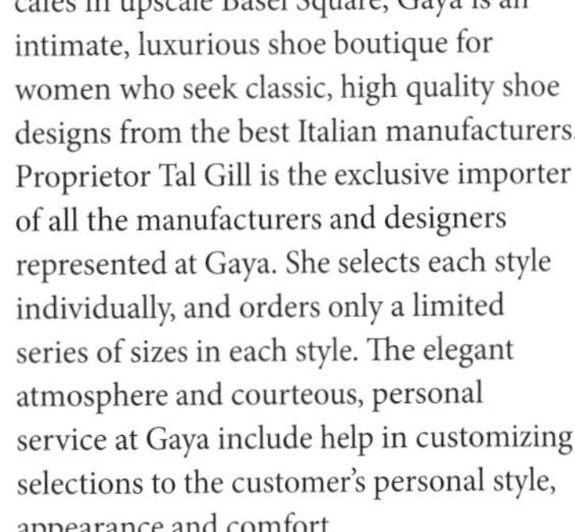

Appropriately located on a quiet street lined with chic jewelry boutiques and charming cafés in upscale Basel Square, Gaya is an intimate, luxurious shoe boutique for women who seek classic, high quality shoe designs from the best Italian manufacturers. Proprietor Tal Gill is the exclusive importer of all the manufacturers and designers represented at Gaya. She selects each style individually, and orders only a limited series of sizes in each style. The elegant atmosphere and courteous, personal service at Gaya include help in customizing selections to the customer's personal style, appearance and comfort.

[Map 10]

[Map 11]

Night

Eliezer

186 Ben Yehuda St.
Tel. (03) 527 5961

This cozy, two-level neighborhood bar is a popular local hangout that personifies the really real Tel Aviv – particularly during the small hours, after most bars and restaurants have closed. Eliezer's secret is simple: a home-like but dynamic atmosphere; good music; a warm welcome for all and a personal welcome for the many regulars; and genuinely good, imaginatively prepared food that perfectly complements an evening of drinking, and puts traditional "pub grub" to shame. The piano-shaped bar and comfortable couches encourage an intimate atmosphere that is seductively laid back and sexy.

[Map 12]

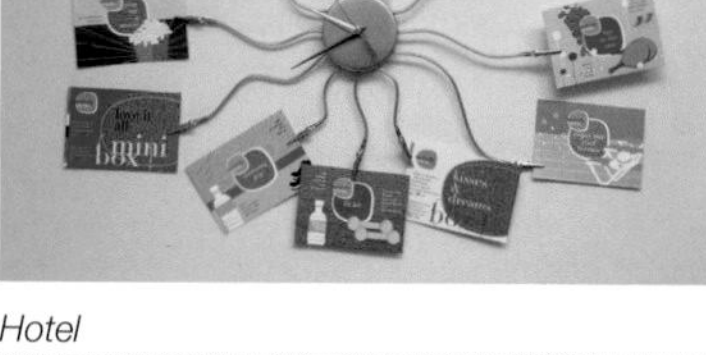

Hotel

Melody Hotel

220 Hayarkon St.
Tel. (03) 521 5300
www.atlas.co.il

The recently renovated Melody Hotel is located directly opposite the beach, within easy walking distance of the north port, Dizengoff Street and Hayarkon Park. With its intimate accommodation, relaxing atmosphere and wide range of business facilities, this stylish 55-room hotel radiates an atmosphere that successfully combines both work and play. The fully air-conditioned rooms have free WiFi, cable television, DVD, a hot beverage corner, refrigerator, direct-dial phone, voicemail and safe (large enough for a laptop). The hotel provides complimentary snacks and beverages in the lobby, as well as a DVD library. The rooftop bar is open during the long summer season.

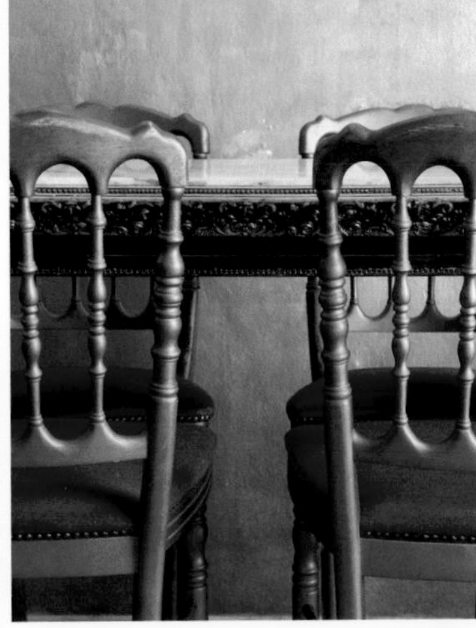

Food

[Map 13]

Agadir Burger Bar

3 Hata'arucha St., Tel Aviv port
Tel. (03) 544 4045
2 Nachalat Binyamin St.
Tel. (03) 510 4442
www.agadir.co.il

Agadir has two enormously popular branches in Tel Aviv – an intimate place on the Nachalat Binyamin pedestrian mall near the Carmel Market, and a larger location near the renovated north port. Both are open until nearly dawn. The huge, juicy gourmet hamburgers, served with a variety of delicious toppings and accompaniments, are widely considered amongst the best in the city. Given that the city is Tel Aviv, where the locals have particularly high standards, it should come as no surprise that the care invested in those burgers is equally reflected in the décor. The tiled floors, warm lighting, heavy wooden bar and banquettes create a cozy atmosphere that is simultaneously nostalgic and modern. There is also an excellent veggie burger.

[Map 14]

Shoes, Bags

Daniella Lehavi

34 Basel St.
Tel. (03) 544 0573
35 Sheinkin St.
Tel. (03) 629 4044
www.daniellalehavi.com

Daniella Lehavi's name is synonymous with luxurious high-end designer products.
Her stylish, high-quality bags, shoes and leather accessories are much sought after by fashionable women, who appreciate both her eye for clean lines and her ability to merge form and function with an elegant touch.
The Swiss-born Israeli designer creates and manufactures most her collections in her own studio and factories, which are located in the greater Tel Aviv area.
Classic and made to last a long time, Daniella Lehavi designs are well worth the investment. Take your time browsing and consulting with the friendly, knowledgeable salespeople – they never pressure their customers to buy, and take genuine pleasure in helping you find what you need.

[Map 15]

'ashion

-rida

90 Dizengoff St.
el. (03) 522 5151
www.frida.co.il

'rida is a seriously talented designer who reates sophisticated, elegant garments for ntelligent women. A graduate of Israel's restigious Shenkar College of Fashion and 'extiles, Frida was chosen from amongst 20 international contenders to compete in he prestigious Italian Mittelmoda Fashion wards. She interned with Donna Karan n New York before returning to Tel Aviv ɔ establish the boutique from which she ells her own designs. While her style is omewhat influenced by her experience vith the famous American designer, Frida's ollections are unmistakably unique. hey are also comfortable, luxurious and attering to a wide range of body types.

[Map 16]

Café

Jeremaiah

306 Dizengoff St., corner of Yermiyahu St.
Tel. (077) 793 1840

In a city famous for its excellent cafés, Jeremaiah is in a class of its own. This cozy, light-filled neighborhood hangout on North Dizengoff aspires successfully to be a second home. The atmosphere is laid back and the food is of the distinctly Israeli home-style variety - meaning that it ranges from Ashkenazi chopped liver to spicy Moroccan fish. The seats are particularly comfortable and the music is never too loud, making Jeremaiah an excellent place to sit for hours and read, chat, work, or use the PlayStation in the upstairs gallery.

Jewelry

Dori Csengeri

242 Dizengoff St.
Tel. (03) 604 3273
www.doricsengeri.com

From Vogue Magazine to the women of Sex and the City, Dori Csengeri's stunning jewelry has illustrated spreads in the most prestigious international fashion publications and decorated the bodies of the world's best-known celebrities. Inspired by fashion and art, and influenced by her background as a textile designer, Dori designs bold, colorful creations that are entirely hand sewn at her atelier, by experienced embroidery craftswomen who are trained in traditional needlework techniques using silky cotton cords. Dori's collections include both spectacular haute couture creations and sophisticated, ready-to-wear pieces that are inset with artful cabochons, fine stones, bohemian and crystal beads. Sensual and surprisingly lightweight, Dori's jewelry is made for chic, elegant women.

[Map 17]

ood

;ushi Samba TLV

7 Habarzel St., Ramat Hachayal
el. (03) 644 4345
ww.sushisamba.com

[Map 18]

)ominated by a huge wall of Mondrian-like olored glass panels, SushiSamba TLV's leek, contemporary bar buzzes with energy ight after night. South American fusion iusic provides a pleasing background) the chatter of the bold and beautiful, s they sip signature cocktails like the :hu-Cucumber, Spicy Ginger and Lemon amurai and nibble appetizers like sashimi nd anticuchos. The vibrant color scheme is epeated in the dining area upstairs, which as a somewhat more low-key vibe. While ushi Samba TLV remains committed to the ignature Brazilian, Japanese and Peruvian uisine that made its New York branch amous, the chef has made the menu even iore eclectic by adding several creative iterpretations of local dishes.

Design

Eretz Israel Museum Shop

Eretz Israel Museum, Tel Aviv
2 Haim Levanon St., Ramat Aviv
Tel. (03) 641 5244 (ext. 8)
www.eretzmuseum.org.il

Located at the entrance to the Eretz Israel Museum, Tel Aviv, the Museum Shop is an enormous, elegant emporium that is known throughout the country for its dedication to the best of traditional and contemporary Israeli decorative arts.

The Museum Shop houses the widest available variety of decorative arts by Israel's most talented artists, many of whose works are sought after by international collectors. The unique contemporary jewelry is selected from the collections of Israel's best-known designers; it is complemented by traditional Yemenite filigree and Roman glass jewelry.

The shop is particularly well known for its collections of ceramic and glass objects, as well as its huge selection of modern and traditional Judaica and holiday items. Additional items include Bedouin embroidery, Ethiopian sculptures, sophisticated children's games that reflect Israeli themes, exhibition catalogues and reproductions of museum artifacts.

[Map 19]

Fashion

Gusta

19 Jabotinsky St. corner of Dizengoff St.
Tel. (077) 323 0038
www.myspace.com/gustastore

Gusta is a quintessentially Tel Aviv boutique. Inspired by young, insouciant local street fashion, designer Ayala Meromi creates clean-lined, casual separates and dresses that are both flattering, edgy interpretations of every day garments sought by women. Ayala's sister, industrial designer Yael Meromi, uses unusual materials to create the bags, wallets, belts and light fixtures displayed throughout the boutique. Various local designers contribute silver jewelry and bags made from recycled materials. In keeping with this ecologically conscious theme, Ayala introduced a line of organic cotton tunics and shirts with artistic graphic prints.

[Map 20]

Café

Café Michal

30 Dizengoff St.
Tel. (03) 523 0236

[Map 21]

Famous for its delicious home-style food, casually friendly service and cozy, upscale Bohemian décor, Café Michal is one of the best and most popular cafes in Tel Aviv. Its regular patrons include famous artists, actors and writers, but Michal maintains a friendly, unpretentious neighborhood atmosphere. Orit, Michal's sister, is a talented cook who creates upscale Israeli comfort food, like stuffed peppers, flavorful soups and poppy seed cake, with a golden touch. Dominic, a French pastry chef, makes the flaky croissants and pastries that go beautifully with a perfectly prepared espresso.

[Map 22]

Jewelry

Yael Herman Gallery

211 Dizengoff St.
Tel. (03) 522 1816
(052) 367 6647
www.yaelherman.com

Yael Herman displays her jewelry designs in a stark white space that gives one the distinct impression of being in an art gallery. This is the intended effect. The artist/designer creates contemporary jewelry in simple geometric forms composed of 24k and 18k gold, silver, stainless steel and diamonds, using a combination of modern technology and traditional craftsmanship. Each design is a three-dimensional sculpture that becomes part of the wearer's personality and spirit. Herman's work has been featured at major international exhibitions, including COLLECT at London's Victoria and Albert Museum, SOFA Art Fair New York and Sienna Gallery MA. Her current collection is called "Stone Garden." Inspired by Zen philosophy, it is about experiencing beauty in the purest and most direct way. Pure gold and a pierced naked diamond, effortlessly floating from stainless steel wire, recreate the tranquillity and serenity of nature.

More of the Best

Café

Alkalay

1 Alkalay St.
Tel. (03) 604 1260

Alkalay is a quiet, unpretentious neighborhood café with a wine shop next door that is owned by the same proprietors.

Fashion

Anny & Adi Jacobson

224 Ben Yehuda St.
Tel. (03) 544 2444

Anny and Adi Jacobson are a husband-and-wife design team who create romantic designs for women. The shop is beautiful, and so are the clothes.

Design

Armani Casa

3 Hata'arucha St.
Tel. (03) 544 3306

Giorgio Armani furniture and home accessories brings Italian style to Tel Aviv. Based on the shop's success, it appears that there are plenty of people in the city who can afford it.

Fashion

Banker

210 Dizengoff St.
Tel. (03) 529 0358

For chic and funky European styles, head for this super-stylish two-floor boutique on north Dizengoff.

Night, Food

Bar Barbunia

192 Ben Yehuda St.
Tel. (03) 524 0961

Laughter and a pervasive joie de vivre are a permanent feature of this popular bar and seafood restaurant on northern Ben Yehuda Street. The place is nearly always crowded, but on Fridays the old-time regulars join the weekend crowd, creating a dense crowd around the bar area as everyone vies for an opportunity to order delicious, simple seafood dishes accompanied by beer on tap and whiskey.

Food

Beta Pizza

3 Hata'arucha St., Tel Aviv port
Tel. 1 599 509 090

If Italian tourists go to Beta for their pizza fix, you know it must be the best in town. The thin crusts and gourmet toppings are irresistible, and there are salads and pasta dishes as well. The prompt, efficient delivery service makes Beta a fantastic option if you're planning on staying in tonight.

Food

Boya

3 Hata'arucha St., Tel Aviv port
Tel. (03) 544 6166

Boya has been around for nearly a decade, and is still as popular as ever. The food is good, the bartenders are experts and the view of the Mediterranean is gorgeous, so what's not to like?

Tabac, Cigars

Brill Cigars

194 Dizengoff St.
Tel. (03) 527 0707

Every sophisticated city has to have at least one luxury emporium for expensive, imported cigars.

Shoes

Couple Of

207 Dizengoff St.
Tel. (03) 529 1098

The shoes at this chic designer shop are unique and beautiful.

Tabac, cigars

Devidas

1 Yehuda Hamaccabi St.
Tel. (03) 602 1602

Most sophisticated cities have at least two luxury emporiums for expensive, imported cigars.

Yoga

Ella Yoga

Hangar 4, Tel Aviv port
Tel. (03) 544 4881

All the different styles of yoga are taught at Ella Yoga. Classes of varying lengths are taught from morning until night, in order to accommodate busy modern schedules. The view and waterfront setting are spectacular.

Night

Erlich

3 Hata'arucha St., Tel Aviv port
Tel. (03) 546 6728

It's a mega bar, it's a pick up bar, it's loud, it's crazy. This is not the place to have a quiet conversation over cocktails with your best friend. It is, however, a great place to cut loose and pick up on Tel Aviv's frenetic energy. Try to avoid coming here on weekends, unless you really enjoy being squashed against a wall.

Fashion

Gertrud

225 Dizengoff St.
Tel. (03) 546 7747

The clothes and lingerie at Gertrud are very chic, very attractive, and very expensive.

Food

Gilly's

Hangar 25, Tel Aviv port
Tel. (03) 605 7777

Originally from Jerusalem, Gilly's is particularly well known for its unconventional breakfasts. The waterfront setting and view are lovely.

Jewelry

H. Stern

Hilton Tel Aviv Hotel
Tel. (03) 524 9619

H. Stern is Israel's best known purveyor of high quality jewelry, with branches all over the world. For years they have maintained the highest standards in quality, innovation and elegance.

Hotel

Hilton Tel Aviv

Independence Garden
Tel. (03) 520 2222

The Hilton Tel Aviv offers all the amenities one would expect of a five-star luxury hotel with an international reputation for excellence.

Ice cream, Pizza

Iceberg Vulcano

Fountain Square, between Hangars 11 and 13, Tel Aviv Port
Tel. (03) 602 6000

Presided over by Chef Yaron Laurent, formerly of l'Arpege in Paris, the staff in the open kitchen produce delicious pizzas and homemade ice cream using classic Italian methods and the freshest, highest quality ingredients. The food is excellent, but the acoustics can drive you a bit cuckoo on Saturday afternoons, when parents bring their noisy children.

Café

Idelson 10

252 Ben Yehuda St.
Tel. (03) 544 4154

This charming little café has fantastic homemade cakes and pastries. If you are in the neighborhood and hungry for breakfast, this is the place to stop.

Café

Lulu Café Patisserie

5 Alkalay St.
Tel. (057) 737 0443

Ladies who lunch love Alkalay for its upscale café menu, polite service and elegant décor. This is a lovely place to linger over a book and a coffee.

Beauty

Miki Buganim Hair Design

1 Pinkas St.
Tel. (03) 546 3242
www.mikibuganim.com

Celebrity makeup artist and hair designer Miki Buganim shot to fame in 1999 when his friend and client, trans gender pop singer Dana International, won the Eurovision contest for Israel. Since then, Buganim has appeared on innumerable television shows as a beauty expert, and done the hair and makeup for countless magazine covers and multi-page spreads of Israel's most famous models and actresses. He specializes in elaborate hair and makeup for brides and bridal parties

Maternity fashion

Motherland

38 Basel St.
Tel. (03) 546 0611

The maternity clothes at this Basel Square boutique are elegant and stylish. They are also rather pricey, but women will always pay a bit more to look beautiful and the garments here are well worth the investment.

Café

Moving Café

308 Dizengoff St.
Tel. (03) 544 4434

Moving is a veteran neighborhood café that is also a DVD library.

Food

Mul Yam

Hangar 24, Tel Aviv port
Tel. (03) 546 9920
www.mulyam.com

This French-Mediterranean haute cuisine restaurant is widely considered one of the best in the country.

Jewelry

Padani

26 Hei Beiyar St., Kikar Hamedina
Tel. (03) 695 1254

Padani has a rock-solid reputation for expensive, high-quality, albeit conventional, jewelry design.

Pilates

Pilates by Dalia Mantver

62 Hei Beiyar St., Kikar Hamedina
Tel. (03) 544 5344
www.mantver-pilates.co.il

Dalia Mantver was one of the first Pilates teachers in Israel. Today she has plenty of competitors, but she is still considered one of the best.

Night

Rosa Parks

256 Dizengoff St.

Rosa Parks looks like a simple neighborhood bar, but for some reason it is one of the most popular places in town. Go figure. Or go check it out.

Jewelry

Shai Lahover

203 Dizengoff St.
Tel. (03) 523 3887

Shay Lahover's exquisite jewelry has earned him an international reputation for top tier design. His baroque, handcrafted pieces are molded from 22 and 24 karat gold, and set with semi and semi-precious stones.

Food

Shila

182 Ben Yehuda St.
Tel. (03) 522 1224

This bar and seafood restaurant attracts a slightly older, worldly clientele. The Mediterranean-influenced cuisine is a delicious accompaniment for the expertly prepared drinks.

Fashion

Tovale

220 Dizengoff St.
Tel. (03) 524 9929

Tovale has been designing funky, colorful women's fashion for decades, but remains perennially popular.

Fashion

Tovale's

220 Dizengoff St.
Tel. (03) 529 8987

Tovale's daughter Naama Chaisin opened her own design shop next door to her mother's. The clothes for women and children are comfortable, colorful and high quality.

Ice cream

Vanilia

22 Ashtori HaFarchi St.
Tel. (03) 602 0185

The freshly made ice cream at this bright little shop comes in a variety of delicoius flavors.

Fashion

Yosef

213 Dizengoff St.
Tel. (03) 529 8998

Yosef designs gorgeous, extraordinary avantgarde evening gowns for women.

Café

Zorik

4 Yehuda Hamaccabi St.
Tel. (03) 604 8858

It's really just a cozy neighborhood café, but we like it.

Café

37

37 Basel St.
Tel. (03) 546 7701

The owners of Shine, one of Tel Aviv's perennially chic cafés, recently opened this super-cool café/restaurant/bar. The menu offers a nod to healthy style food with entrées that include tofu and brown rice, but the attitude seems to be that hip is good for you, too. The coffee is great and there's a happening bar scene every night.

City **Center**

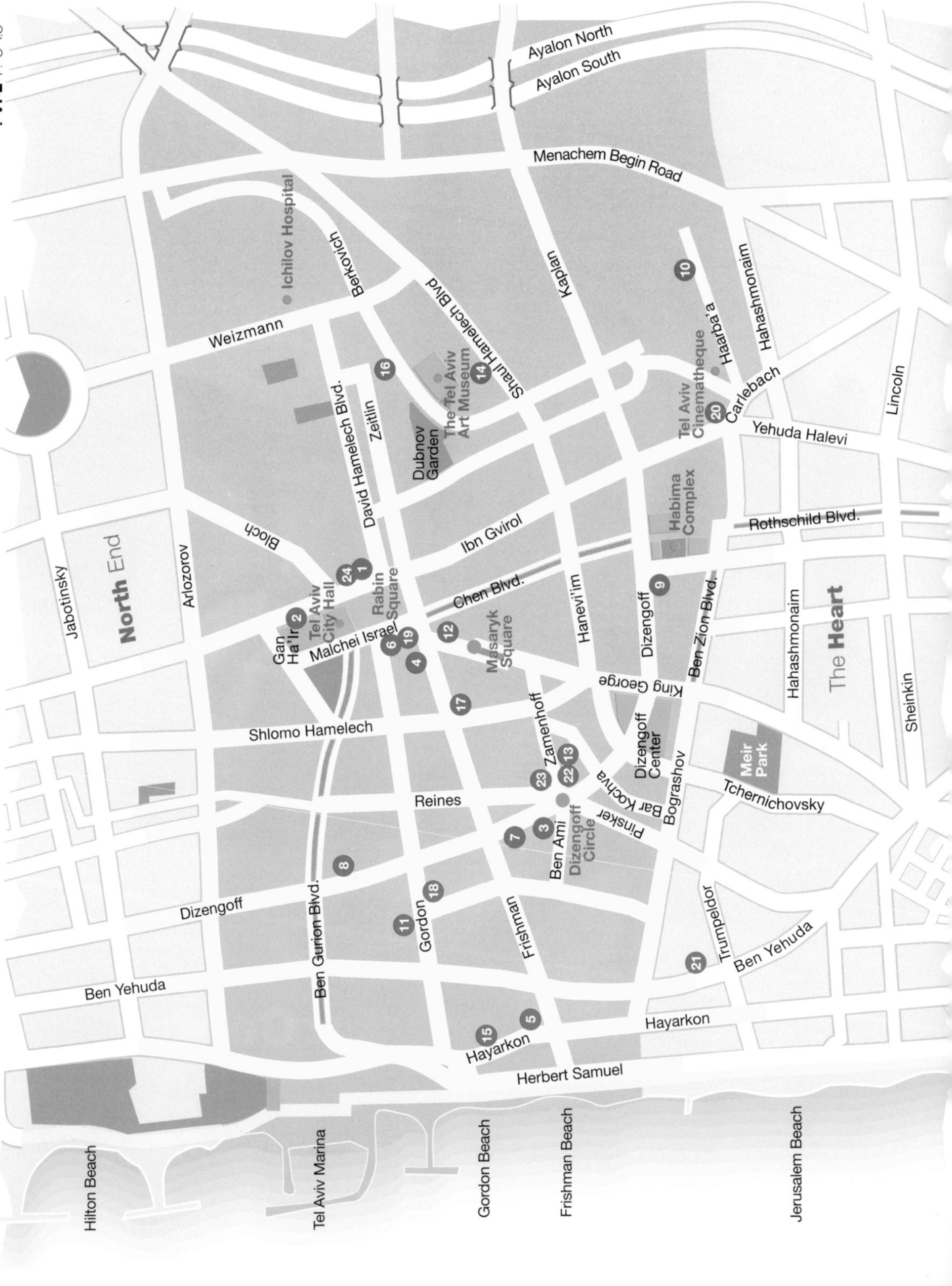

Ayalon North
Ayalon South
Menachem Begin Road
Ichilov Hospital
Berkovich
Shaul Hamelech Blvd
Kaplan
Hahashmonaim
10
Weizmann
The Tel Aviv Art Museum
14
16
Tel Aviv Cinematheque
Haarba'a
Carlebach
20
Lincoln
Yehuda Halevi
David Hamelech Blvd.
Zeitlin
Dubnov Garden
Habima Complex
Rothschild Blvd.
Bloch
Ibn Gvirol
Jabotinsky
North End
Arlozorov
24
1
Rabin Square
Chen Blvd.
Hanevi'im
Dizengoff
9
Ben Zion Blvd.
Hahashmonaim
The **Heart**
Gan Ha'Ir
2
Tel Aviv City Hall
Malchei Israel
6
19
4
12
Masaryk Square
King George
Sheinkin
17
Shlomo Hamelech
Zamenhoff
13
22
23
Dizengoff Center
Bograshov
Meir Park
Tchernichovsky
Reines
Bar Kochva
Pinsker
7
3
Ben Ami
Dizengoff Circle
8
18
Gordon
11
Dizengoff
Frishman
Trumpeldor
21
Ben Yehuda
Ben Yehuda
Ben Gurion Blvd.
5
15
Hayarkon
Hayarkon
Herbert Samuel
Hilton Beach
Tel Aviv Marina
Gordon Beach
Frishman Beach
Jerusalem Beach

City Center

The center of Tel Aviv is a sprawling area that includes many of its major institutions. It is home to the Israel Philharmonic Orchestra and Habimah, the national theater; to the Tel Aviv Museum of Art, the New Israeli Opera and the main branch of the municipal library; to the multi-story municipality building, the courthouses, plenty of stylish boutiques; three shopping malls; and several well-known cafés and restaurants. It contains lots of squares – Rabin Square, Dizengoff Square, Masaryk Square (although only one of them is actually square-shaped) plus three boulevards and a marina. Most of the residential sections in the center of the city are considered upscale, although this is due more to location than aesthetics.

Some sections of central Tel Aviv were "uglified" during the 1970s. Dizengoff Square and Kikar Atarim are prime examples of what can kindly be called "errors in urban planning" – or less kindly, urban blight. The eastern section of Shaul Hamelech (King Saul) Boulevard, on the other hand, received a facelift during the 1990s. Still other areas were left untouched – kept very much as they were in the 1940s, albeit much in need of renovation.

Central Tel Aviv is not the most beautiful or historic area of the city, although there are many examples of International style architecture on the side streets. It is, however, an integral part of the city, and an excellent place to experience its rhythm and lifestyle.

Central **Dizengoff** St.

From the early 1950s through mid-1970s, central Dizengoff was one of the city's most stylish places to gather in cafes, shop and stroll. This is also where Israel's most famous poets, authors and journalists gathered at now-defunct cafes that were once household names. The verb "lehizdangef," from the name Dizengoff, was coined to describe a stroll along Tel Aviv's longest street. Decades later, the verb has become an anachronism and central Dizengoff is no longer the most stylish area in the city, but it is still a busy hub of activity that offers lots of opportunities for eating, drinking, shopping and people watching.

Dizengoff Square, the neglected, slightly seedy, round pedestrian bridge with the monstrous colored fountain in the middle, is one of the primary examples of ugly 1970s Tel Aviv architecture. Internationally renowned kinetic sculptor Yaacov Agam, who recently had a European retrospective, won a competition to design the fountain, which was supposed to symbolize fire and water. The municipality's intentions were good – they wanted to allow easier flow of traffic below the bridge while contributing to the city's cultural heritage.

Unfortunately, there was never enough money to maintain the square with the fountain, and it has now become one of the biggest controversies in Tel Aviv. There is a plan to destroy and rebuild it, but no agreement on how the rebuilding should be handled; many want the original square, which was at ground level, to be restored – but that would create enormous traffic problems. The controversy is illustrative of the passion Tel Avivians feel for their city, as well as their conflicting visions.

The bridge did kill off most of the commercial activity on this section of Dizengoff. Now it is a popular nighttime gathering place for teenage punk rockers, while during the day it is a place where old people stop to rest during their daily walks, or where buskers perform to earn a few shekels. On Tuesdays and Fridays there is a flea market under the bridge. If you're looking for a 1970s LP of a long-forgotten pop singer, or a cut-glass candy dish that looks like the one your grandmother had, this is the place to shop.

60 Dizengoff **Center**

Dizengoff Center, Israel's first shopping mall, was built in the 1970s at the corner of King George and Dizengoff. It has long been surpassed in elegance and variety by the newer shopping malls in Tel Aviv's northern suburbs, but it is a popular and convenient place to shop for a wide, if standard, selection of clothes, household goods and groceries. Dizengoff Center is a classic example of Israeli 1970s "ugly architecture," but it has a nice, comfortable vibe that feels very communal – much more like an outdoor shopping area than a sterile, enclosed mall.

The mall contains branches of almost all the popular fast food restaurants, including Israel's homegrown coffee chains, plus two multiplex cinemas. The Lev cinema on the uppermost floor is more of an art-house cinema, while the cinema on the lowest floor screens current Hollywood releases.

On Fridays there is a popular international food fair at Dizengoff Center. The

corridors of the mall are lined with an astonishing variety of cooked food, from Moroccan to Chinese.

Ben Gurion Blvd.

Named for Israel's first prime minister, Ben Gurion Boulevard is mostly residential and somewhat neglected-looking. But visitors still come to visit David Ben Gurion's boxy white house, now a museum, and the boulevard is a pleasant connecting path between the beach and Rabin Square. It is popular with strollers and has some "interesting" modern sculptures by local artists on the stretch between Dizengoff and the beach.

Which brings us to the second example of horrible 1970s municipal planning - Kikar Atarim. The neglected, breathtakingly ugly square at the foot of the boulevard overlooks the beach and the marina; unfortunately, the view is Atarim's only redeeming feature. Originally planned as a shopping mall, Atarim was left semi-complete and is a true eyesore. A few over-priced tourist restaurants serving greasy, semi-edible Israeli-style fast food and beers populate the square. As with the Dizengoff pedestrian bridge, there are yet-to-be-realized plans to renovate Kikar Atarim – as soon as the funding is found and an agreement between the residents and the municipality reached. Winter or summer, and barring a driving rainstorm, each Saturday afternoon there is folk dancing on the pavement beneath the stairs that lead down to the beach.

The beach here is relatively quiet, and the marina, with its sparkling, luxurious yachts, is lovely to look at. Since Tel Aviv is blessed with sunny weather on most days, you might want to buy an ice cream, sit down on a bench and spend some time contemplating the view.

Ben Zion Blvd., **Chen** Blvd., **Masaryk** Square, and **Rabin** Square

Habimah, the complex that houses Israel's national theater is undergoing extensive renovations as of this writing. It is the connecting point between Ben Zion and Chen Boulevards, which run roughly perpendicular to one another. Neither is important in terms of architecture, history or monuments, but they are leafy, sedate, largely residential and lovely for strolling or bicycling.

Chen Boulevard leads from Habimah to Rabin Square. It is lined with tree-shaded benches that are nearly always occupied by a typical cross-section of the neighborhood's population - ranging from infirm octogenarians accompanied by their caregivers, to mothers with babies. The boulevard is quiet on most days, but when there is a major event at Rabin Square it is packed with people. The significance of Rabin Square lies in its history and purpose - not in its design. Originally called Kings of Israel, the square was renamed after the late Prime Minister Yitzhak Rabin was assassinated at a peace rally held on the site. A monument, including a diagram of Rabin's last movements, is beneath the steps of the municipality. Israelis gather at Rabin Square to celebrate, to mourn and to listen to live performances. It is a national monument of the best kind – a living one that is well used.

Located just a few steps from Rabin Square, Masaryk Square (which is really a circle) is named for Thomas Masaryk, the first president of Czechoslovakia. Over the past few years several local designers have opened boutiques around the square, contributing a chic and fashionable atmosphere. There are also several good cafés, mostly overlooking the little square with the fountain. Masaryk has a truly local atmosphere – one of laid-back, Tel Aviv-style, urban chic. It is a very pleasant place to shop, wander and linger over coffee.

Ben Zion Boulevard leads from Habimah down to King George Street, where it morphs into Bograshov Street and continues on to the beach. If you are heading for Dizengoff Center, just turn right at King George and continue to the next corner. The intersection of King George and Bograshov tends to be noisy and hectic, but if you really need a break, there's a fairly good café on one of the corners – or you could stop in and browse at the Third Ear CD shop and DVD library. There is a small cinema on the third floor, where excellent local documentary films are screened daily. Check the posters on the front door for details, or ask the staff in the DVD library on the second floor.

Gan Ha'ir and **Ibn Gvirol** St.

Just behind the municipality building is the upscale Gan Ha'ir (City Garden) shopping mall. When it first opened in the 1980s, Gan Ha'ir was considered the most elite shopping center in the city. This is not the case anymore. There

tel aviv museum

C.F.H.
1873.

are still several elegant and expensive shops at Gan Ha'ir, and it does cling to its elite image, but the atmosphere is an aging one. This is perhaps best illustrated by the Hungarian café, Yehudith's (Judith's). With its clusters of German-and-Hungarian-speaking octogenarian ladies consuming coffee with whipped cream and strudel, Yehudíth's feels like pre-war Mitteleuropa – a real time machine. The food is mediocre at best, the coffee is worse and the service is grouchy, but Yehudith's aging clientele remains loyal nonetheless.

The section of Ibn Gvirol Street facing the municipality is a hodgepodge of businesses that range from fashionable boutiques to dim, old-fashioned shops selling orthopedic shoes and thermal undies. The street is, however, evolving very rapidly lately. The municipality recently widened and improved the road, and fashionable shops, cafés and restaurants are replacing the dusty, old-fashioned, family run businesses. Despite the cacophony produced by the diesel buses and honking taxi drivers, Ibn Gvirol is a pleasant place to stroll, have coffee and browse the shops.

The area around Dubnov Street, which runs in a vaguely parallel line to Ibn Gvirol, is considered upscale – but mostly for its population rather than its architectural value. Designed and built during the 1950s to woo the wealthy American Jews who never did get around to immigrating, it has a garden city look, with generous plots of land and lots of green areas surrounding the residences, as well as a large, well-maintained park.

Shaul Hamelech Blvd.

Shaul Hamelech Boulevard feels big and impersonal. It lacks the charm of the narrower, tree-lined boulevards and is far more traffic-clogged. But this is where the Tel Aviv Museum of Modern Art is located, as well as the new structure housing the New Israeli Opera, the main branch of the municipal public library and an art-house cinema. The Museum of Modern Art is not a particularly lovely building, but it has some very good permanent and temporary exhibitions. Many of Israel's most famous artists exhibit here. For children, there are interactive exhibitions and live performances.

Carlebach, Hahashmonaim and **Haarba'a** Sts.

The Cinematheque, the city's main art house cinema, is set in a leafy square on Sprinzak Street, where Hahashmonaim, Haarba'a and Carlebach intersect. The square is lined with benches and shaded by trees, making it a very pleasant place to sit. The cinema itself screens a wide variety of art-house films from all over the world, including cult films and Israeli underground hits. There is a bilingual schedule available both online and in the lobby; the latter houses a café where live jazz is performed on Friday afternoons.

Haarba'a Street is lined with good restaurants that range from sushi to pub grub. It is a popular destination for both business lunches and a night out on the town.

Hahashmonaim Street is undergoing major changes. For years one side was lined with falafel joints, shops and restaurants, while the other was primarily a big, dirty open lot, occupied by the wholesale fruit and vegetable market. Recently the municipality decided to move the market to make room for a major luxury housing development. Construction has already begun on this controversial project – yet more evidence of how quickly Tel Aviv is expanding.

Carlebach is named after Azriel Carlebach, the founding editor of Maariv newspaper. The Maariv building still stands in its original location, looking much the worse for wear, and the rest of the street is quite unattractive. There are a couple of mediocre cafés, a pub or two and a popular karaoke club, where middle-aged types come to sing old Hebrew folk songs, but otherwise Carlebach is the kind of street you won't regret missing.

Azrieli Center

The Azrieli Center is one of the best-known landmarks in Tel Aviv. Built in the shapes of a circle, a square and a triangle, the Azrieli towers were, for a very brief period, the tallest in the Middle East – until Dubai's massive construction boom left Tel Aviv in the dust. The first three floors of the center are occupied by a pretty generic, American-style shopping mall, complete with multiplex, luxury health club and junk food outlets, that has no uniquely Israeli characteristics. The main reason to visit the Azrieli Center is for the spectacular, panoramic view from the observation platform on the 49th floor. On a clear day you can see all up and down the coast, and as far eastward as the Judean Hills.

Sarona Garden

Directly opposite the Azrieli Center is the recently restored Sarona Garden. Once a Templar Colony that was an agricultural village, Sarona was established in 1871 by German religious pilgrims who settled in the Holy Land. The single story homes made of stone are classic Templar structures; and for years they were left to crumble from neglect. Recently, the municipality recognized their architectural value and restored them. The plan is to turn the Sarona area into a commercial area that combines new buildings with the restored Templar structures, with tree-lined paths and outdoor cafes completing the sense of an urban oasis. The plans show that great attention has been paid to preserving the original trees and to combining old and new with respect to both the past and the future.

Food, Night

Brasserie M&R

70 Ibn Gvirol St.
Tel. (03) 696 7111

From its meticulously detailed Art Deco interior to its nicotine stained tiled ceiling and hardwood floors, the Brasserie is a paean to the traditional Parisian grand brasserie. Open 24 hours in the spirit of Brasserie Lip and La Coupoule, this Tel Aviv landmark is one of the city's most popular drinking and dining spots.

The Brasserie is regularly listed as one of the best restaurants in the country. Critics invariably praise the creative, iconoclastic cuisine, which includes perfectly prepared, classic brasserie fare such as steak tartar, braised short ribs, choucroute garni and boeuf bourgignon, as well as lighter Mediterranean fare and Israeli favorites like goat cheese salad and shakshuka. The unifying factors – and the source of the restaurant's broad appeal - are impeccable preparation and excellent service.

The Brasserie is packed 'round the clock, although the atmosphere changes according to the time of day (or night). The clientele includes an Israeli Who's Who that ranges from diplomats, politicians and journalists - to pop stars, models and actors. They come for relaxed brunches, power lunches, early evening drinks and late dinners. Most of all, they come for the food, which never disappoints.

[Map 1]

Le Bar à Huîtres
PETIT
DÉJEUNER

[Map 2]

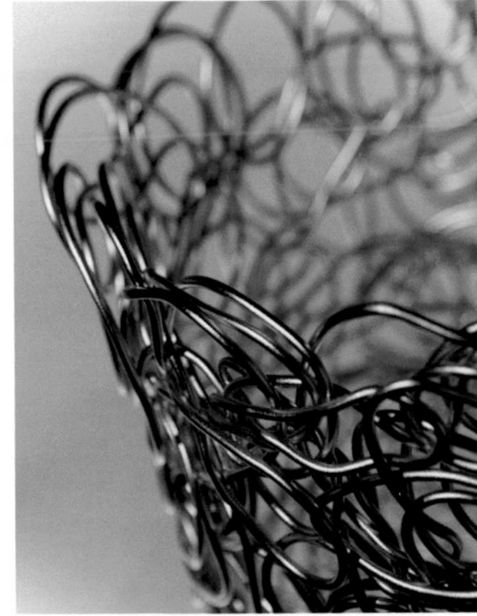

Design

Tollman's

71 Ibn Gvirol St.,
Gan Ha'Ir shopping complex
Tel. (03) 522 3236
www.tollmans.co.il

Tollman's has the exclusive representation in Israel of more than 30 leading international designers of contemporary home & garden furnishings, accessories and cooking appliances. The sleek, elegant and uncompromisingly modern kitchen and dining accessories on display at Tollman's showrooms bear prestigious international brand names such as Cassina, Cappellini, Edra, Giorgetti , Poltronafrau, Minotti, Molteni, Alessi, Dedon, Dada, Le Creuset, Dibbern and Kalla .

The top international designers whose innovative creations are regularly displayed at Tollman's include style groundbreakers such as Philipe Starck, Patricia Urquiola, Karim Rashid, Jasper Morrison, Tom Dixon, Stefano Giovannoni and Le Corbusier. For stylish Israelis with excellent taste and a comfortable budget, Tollman's is an essential shopping destination.

Since the original branch of Tollman's opened more than 20 years ago, Israel's top architects and interior designers have relied on the shop's buyers to maintain a wide variety of the absolute best in prestigious international designs in furniture and accessories for the homes of their elite clientele. Once considered de rigueur, European buying trips are no longer necessary. The Tel Aviv branch of Tollman's opened two years ago in Gan Ha'Ir, the city's most luxurious shopping center. The beautiful displays and helpful, knowledgeable staff make it a truly pleasurable shopping experience.

Café, DVD, Laundry

dizi

13 Ben Ami St., Dizengoff Square
Tel. (03) 629 4559
www.dizi.co.il

Enjoy a meal or coffee, surf the 'net, do your laundry or watch a film and meet Tel Aviv locals – you can do it all simultaneously at dizi, a fabulous concept café located just off Dizengoff Square, opposite the Rav Hen multiplex.

Dizi is the ultimate solution for travelers that like to do everything with style – even mundane chores like laundry. The café, with its varied brunch options, sandwiches, salads, entrées, cakes and gourmet coffee, divides the spotless launderette from the DVD library, which stocks an intelligent selection of Hollywood blockbusters, domestic films and international art-house flicks. You can throw your dirty clothes in one of the machines, then lounge on the comfortable couch while surfing the 'net via the free WiFi or watching a DVD, accompanied by a meal and coffee. Laptops can also be rented by the hour.

[Map 3]

Food Boutique

Olia

73 Frishman St.
Tel. (03) 522 3235
www.olia.co.il

[Map 4]

Olia is a paean to the olives of Israel. This charming boutique draws in passersby with its striking design, seducing them with its flavors and scents.

Nine varieties of custom-bottled Israeli olive oil are displayed on shelves painted in Olia's trademark red and green color scheme, with the provenance and unique qualities of each oil lovingly described on laminated cards. Olia also stocks its own olives, tapenades, spice blends and herbal tea infusions.

All are local, in keeping with Olia's active involvement in promoting the philosophy of the international Slow Food movement. There is even a selection of Olia's own, locally made, olive oil-based soaps and cosmetic products.

While the emphasis is on olive-related products nurtured in Israel, Olia also imports high-quality items from around the Mediterranean region. These include hand-infused oils from Italy's Liguria region, and a variety of French specialty vinegars.

Hotel

Prima Tel Aviv

105 Hayarkon St.
Tel. (03) 520 6666
www.prima.co.il

Prima Tel Aviv is a boutique hotel that combines style, intimacy, excellent service and a central location. It is one of Tel Aviv's most popular choices for discerning travelers, whether they are visiting for work or for leisure. There are conference rooms for business travelers, and an art gallery featuring Israeli artists. The beach is right on the hotel's doorstep, while Dizengoff Street can be reached on foot within five minutes. Prima Tel Aviv's minimalist, modern décor radiates comfort and tranquility, while design references celebrate Tel Aviv's style and history. During the evenings, candles are lit in the lobby, while relaxing music plays in the background. Pre-dinner drinks can be enjoyed in the chic bar area, with its flattering lighting and attentive bartenders.

[Map 5]

ashion

Mayu

Malchei Israel St., Rabin Square
el. (03) 527 3992
dditional branch:
1 Ussishkin St., Ramat HaSharon
el. (03) 549 9033

Vhen she established the first branch of Mayu in Rabin Square, pioneering designer Maya Zukerman established the roots of he flowering contemporary local fashion cene in the immediate area. While she sells he same collections at each branch, the ocus on color varies, as does the variety f accessories. The Rabin Square branch ncludes private collections by Israeli nd foreign designers chosen by Maya Zukerman. Mayu's rapid proliferation s testimony to the designer's deep nderstanding of the city's Zeitgeist and ashion outlook. She expresses it perfectly vith her collections of casual and style-conscious clothes and accessories that are exy in an appealingly understated manner. The fabrics are all natural fibers – primarily otton and wool – that breathe, making hem well suited to the long, hot and humid ummers. They also work beautifully as ayers during the brief, but chilly and damp, rainy season.

[Map 6]

Design

Bauhaus Center

99 Dizengoff St.
Tel. (03) 522 0249
www.bauhaus-center.com

The Bauhaus Center sells a wide variety of well-chosen books on the history of the city and the Bauhaus School, historical posters (prints and originals), and contemporary designs by local artists. Changing exhibitions about the history and art of Tel Aviv are displayed in the upstairs gallery. The Center also leads tours of Tel Aviv's Bauhaus history on Friday mornings, starting at 10 o'clock. A map and recorded self-guided tour (in English, French and Hebrew) is available for those who prefer to do the tour on alternate days.

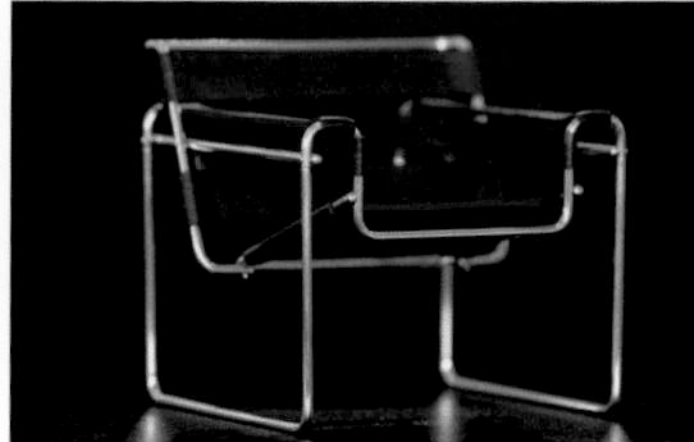

[Map 7]

[Map 8]

Fashion

Sarah Braun

162 Dizengoff St.
Tel. (03) 529 9902

Sarah Braun creates whimsical, individualistic designs with a slightly retro feel. Her collections are designed for active women with a strong sense of individual style, a sense of humor and an appreciation for multi-function garments that are suitable for day and evening wear. The collections tend to be small, but each item reflects the designer's commitment to detail and high quality. The color range is purposely monochromatic, ranging from shades of gray to shades of black, to maximize their wearability. Sarah Braun's collections have been widely praised by Israeli fashion critics.

Eyewear

Claude Samuel

17 Dizengoff St.
Tel. (03) 620 8882

[Map 9]

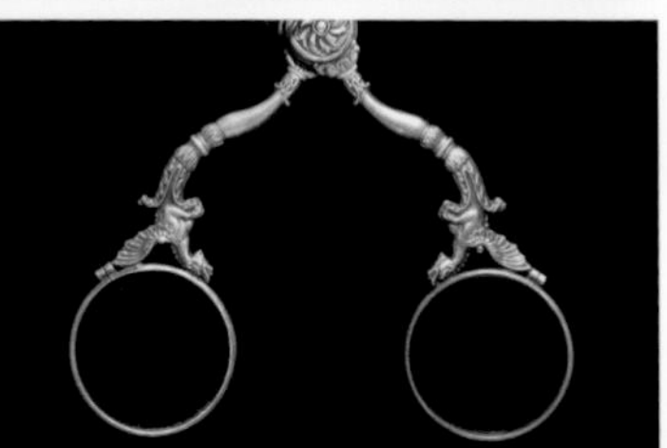

Claude Samuel's optometry clinic and gallery boutique radiates professionalism, courtesy and elegance. A smiling receptionist serves espresso to waiting patients; inevitably one spends the brief waiting period perusing the striking eyeglass frames displayed along the walls. Descended from a French family that has been prominent optometrists since 1848, Mr. Samuel is a senior optometrist at Tel Hashomer Hospital, a position he has held for two decades. He bases his thorough eye examinations on a holistic approach to the eye that goes well beyond a simple vision check. Mr. Samuel then customizes glasses to suit and reflect the personalities of his customers, which include presidents, prime ministers and quite possibly your next-door neighbour.

Recently, Claude Samuel launched his own collection of high-quality, vintage-style eyewear. It is displayed alongside selected imported designs by high-end names such as Anne & Valentin and Beausoleil.

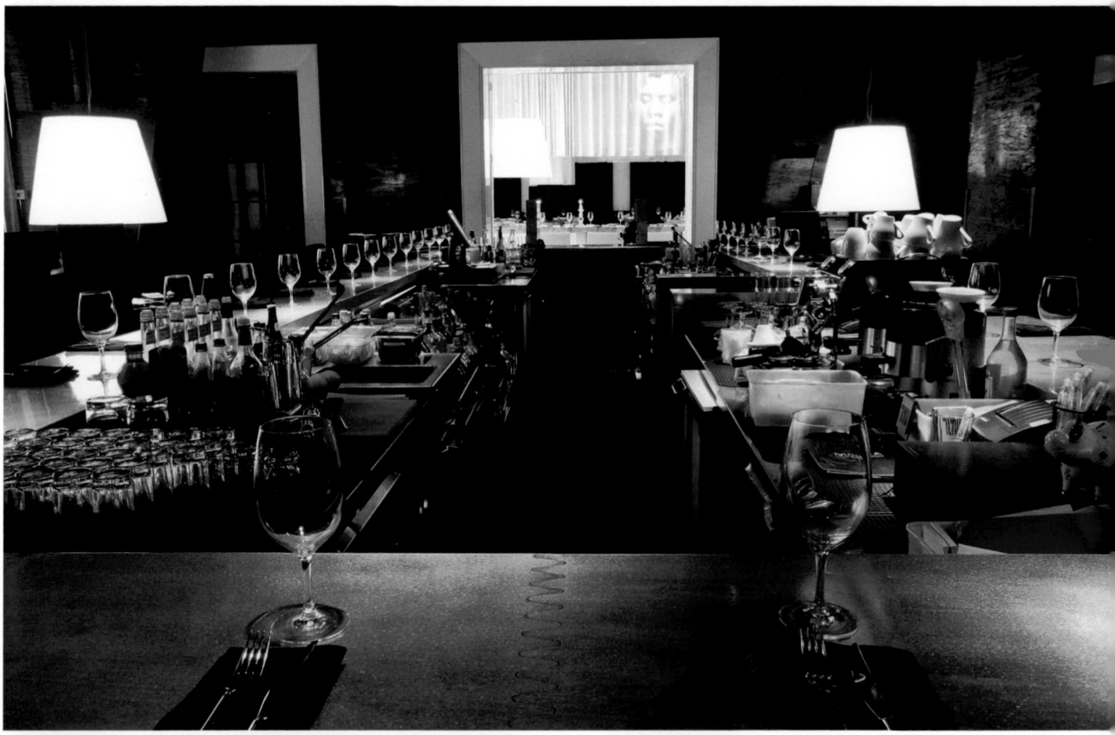

Food, Night

Messa

19 Haarba'a St.
Tel. (03) 685 6859
www.messa.co.il

Messa is the only Israeli restaurant featured in Condé Nast Traveler's list of the world's 80 Great New Restaurants. Chef Aviv Moshe has won praise from critics around the world for his unique, Provençal-influenced cuisine that is, he says, inspired by memories of his mother's kitchen. He updates the menu constantly – depending on the season, locally available ingredients and his mood. Diners are invariably surprised and delighted by the imagination and depth of flavor in each dish. The richly varied drinks menu includes a variety of creative cocktails, expertly prepared and served by a professional bar staff. The intimate, dimly lit bar area is an attractive setting in which to enjoy a pre-dinner drink and sample the offerings of the tasting menu.

/essa has redefined chic dining in Israel vith its striking décor. Designer Alex Aeitlis expertly combines various seating rrangements with a unique interpretation f space that invites both intimacy and ociability. Wallpaper Magazine included Aessa in its list of the 50 most beautiful estaurants in the world.

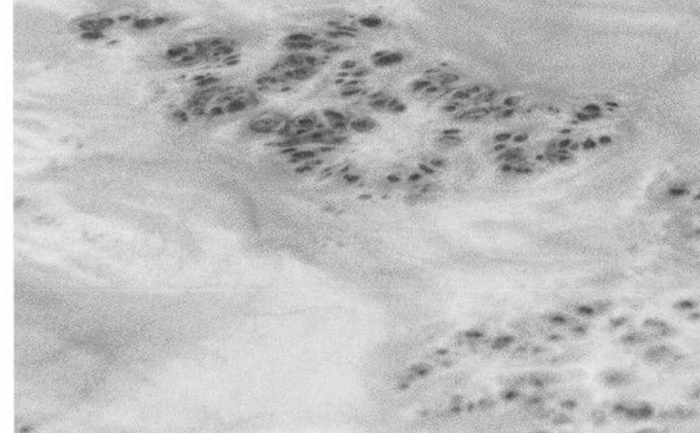

Design

Arbitman's

31 Gordon St.
Tel. (03) 527 8254

Appropriately located on a street lined with art galleries, Arbitman's is a hymn of praise to unique and beautiful design. Proprietor Benny Arbitman, who is one of Israel's best-known theater and film set designers, and an indisputable authority of style and taste, chooses the wide range of items at prestigious markets all over the world – but primarily in Europe.

Arbitman's is divided into four sections, with each dedicated to a different design concept. In the first two are an eclectic collection of objects, composed of a variety of materials, colors and textures. These include Italian glass, Bolivian wood vases and beautiful handmade mobiles. In the Red, Black & White room, enormous vases are displayed alongside unique, handmade bags.

The Time Tunnel is reserved for nostalgia. The wide range of objects here includes rare porcelain, clocks manufactured in the 1970s and gramophones from the 1930s.

Arbitman's sells the works of several well-known Israeli artists, and is also the exclusive representative of Natan Elkanovich, the internationally renowned pop artist.

[Map 11]

Books

Librairie du Foyer

14 Masaryk Square
Tel. (03) 524 3835
www.librairie.co.il

Appropriately nestled between two Parisian-style cafes, Librairie Du Foyer is a cozy French bookshop that has been an institution for Tel Aviv's French speakers since 1968. Proprietor Myriam Ezra, who purchased the shop from the original owners in 2001, stocks a wide range of contemporary and classic French literature and non-fiction. There is also a comprehensive selection of Hebrew titles translated into French, as well as French titles translated into Hebrew. Customers who have only high school French will enjoy the Asterix and Tintin comics and the welcoming, intimate atmosphere.

[Map 12]

Fashion

Tanti Becky

63 Bar Kochva St.,
off Dizengoff St.
Tel. (03) 525 5995

[Map 13]

This hip, young boutique is a family affair: cousins Yael and Hadas, who look like sisters and share an impeccable sense of style, named it for a legendary aunt and designed every detail of the decor themselves. The result is an eclectic, unique, Euro-funky atmosphere that reflects their love of aesthetics and expresses their personal attitude to fashion. The cousins hand select each garment and accessory from the collections of designers who work all over the world – from the Far East to Europe to Israel - choosing only articles that they truly love.

[Map 14]

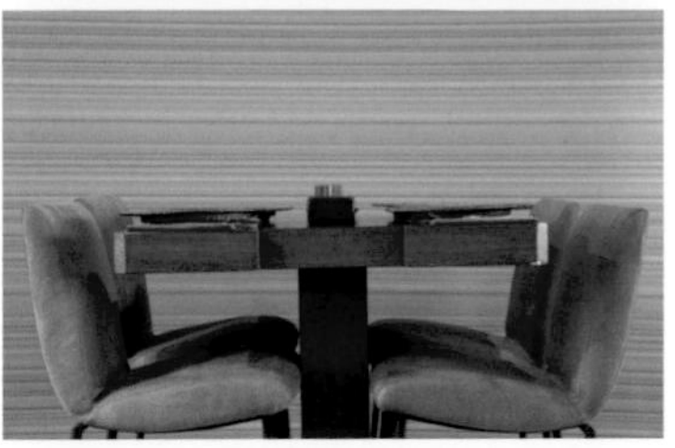

Food

Food Art

23 Shaul Hamelech Blvd.
Tel. (03) 695 0957
www.foodart.co.il

Lunch at Food Art is a truly memorable experience. The food, service and décor at this sophisticated yet relaxing restaurant are all faultless, a fact that is appreciated by its many regular patrons.

Omer Miller, the talented chef, creates seasonal menus that reflect his unique and sophisticated approach to local ingredients. Combining Mediterranean, French and Asian influences, Chef Miller's dishes have deceptively simple sounding names that belie their beautiful presentation and complex flavors. Each course is perfectly proportioned, so as to leave diners feeling satisfied but not sated.

Anner Tzalel, the in-house pastry chef, creates irresistible desserts, ranging from chocolate to fruit confections. Each is lovingly presented and perfectly complements each meal.

The intelligent wine list includes internationally known vintages as well as excellent selections from the best local boutique wineries.

Food Art is open for lunch only. In the evenings, it caters private events.

Hotel

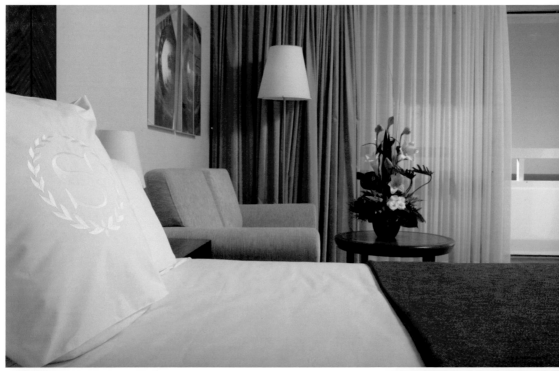

Sheraton Tel Aviv Hotel & Towers

115 Hayarkon St.
Tel. (03) 521 1111
www.sheraton.com/telaviv

[Map 15]

With its combination of luxury, comfort, amenities and central location, the Sheraton Tel Aviv is an excellent choice for sophisticated travelers. Recently renovated, this five-star hotel offers the highest international standards in service and amenities, and is widely considered amongst the best in Israel

The 317 rooms include 22 suites, all furnished and equipped with great attention to detail. These include the Sheraton Sweet Sleeper Bed; deluxe bathroom accessories; 32-inch LCD televisions with cable access and movie on demand; and high-speed Internet access. Working travelers will be particularly satisfied with the full range of services offered by the 24-hour business center.

The hotel has two swimming pools - as well as a spa and gym. The critically praised Olive Leaf Restaurant proves that kosher gourmet dining is not an oxymoron. Pre-dinner drinks can be enjoyed in the bar, with its striking beachfront views.

Food

Toto

4 Berkovich St.
Tel. (03) 693 5151

Since Chef Yaron Shalev took over the kitchen about one year ago, Toto has assumed its place amongst the best restaurants in Israel. Shalev, 25, is a legend in the local culinary scene. He started training at the age of 12, and rapidly worked his way up to sous chef at Tel Aviv's most highly regarded restaurants, under the supervision of Israeli chefs who are practically household names. At Toto he has created a seasonal menu of the best local and imported ingredients, prepared in a style that fuses Italian and Mediterranean culinary influences. With its flattering light, clean lines, comfortable seating and wood accents, Toto radiates casual elegance and quiet luxury. Daily specials are written on the blackboard near the wooden bar, which is popular with patrons who wish to forego a full meal in favor of a pizza or salad accompanied by a glass of wine. There is an intelligent wine list, and the desserts are marvelous.

[Map 17]

Café

Shine

38 Shlomo Hamelech St.
Tel. (03) 527 6186

A favorite gathering place for Tel Aviv's beautiful and fashionable denizens, Shine is one of the city's hippest cafes. The menu includes many whimsical twists on café standards, plus healthy dishes that you'll order simply because they're good eating – like the fabulous tofu salad, a mix of crunchy greens and crispy tofu sticks sautéed in sweet and spicy chili sauce, or the all-day breakfast with soft-boiled eggs and whole-wheat toast. At night the lights are dimmed and Shine becomes a happening bar scene, with delicious house-special cocktails.

Fashion

Oberson Fashion House

36 Gordon St.
Tel. (03) 524 3822
www.oberson.co.il

[Map 18]

Oberson is one of the most prestigious names in the Israeli fashion world. Designer Gideon Oberson has set the gold standard in high-fashion swimwear for more than 40 years. International fashion critics regularly use the word “exquisite” to describe his collections, and many of his loyal customers make regular pilgrimages to Tel Aviv. His is also Israel’s most prestigious name in prêt-à-porter and custom-designed eveningwear. Twenty years ago, his daughter Karen widened the appeal of the Oberson name with her KO label – elegant, high quality, sporty separates and dresses.

Design, Fashion

Nook

5 Malchei Israel St., Rabin Square
Tel. (03) 527 7177
www.nook.co.il

[Map 19]

If Catherine Deneuve and Princess Masako opened a shop together, it would look like Nook. This lovely boutique is a cosmopolitan, eclectic homage to the very best in luxury and style. Combining Parisian joie de vivre and chic with futuristic Japanese modernity and precision, Nook radiates an atmosphere of style and impeccable quality. The selection of items includes exclusive French body and home fragrances; elaborate silk kimonos; and delicate, hand-made jewelry from Holland. The unique fashion pieces are individually selected from the collections of niche designers all over the world.

[Map 20]

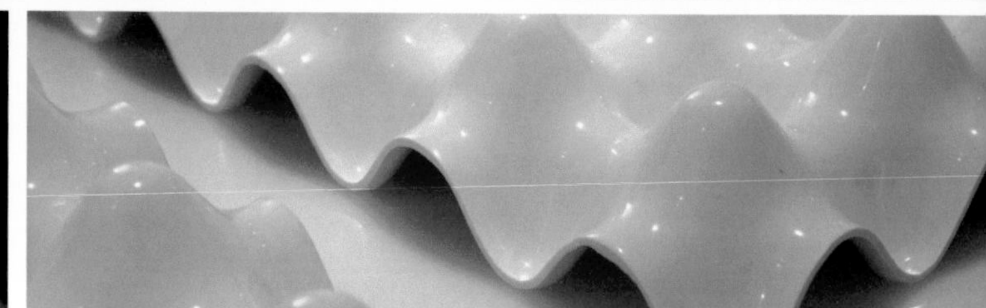

Design

Habitat

2 Ibn Gvirol St.
71 Ibn Gvirol St.
43 Carlebach St.
Tel. (03) 695 1282
www.habitat.co.il

Habitat's three Tel Aviv showrooms are landmarks of elegance and contemporary style. Each focuses on a uniquely edited vision of the very best in modern design for both office and home.

Over the past three decades, owners Rami and Etty Meerovitch have established an international reputation for their knowledge of modern design. Their constantly changing, imported collections represent carefully selected items by the most famous and sought-after names in the field. These range from groundbreaking twentieth-century innovators, such as Ray and Charles Eames and Verner Panton, to designers such as Vico Magistretti, Philippe Starck, Antonio Citterio, Piero Lissoni, Patricia Urquiola and Ron Arad. Famous names in contemporary design include Arclinea, B&B Italia, de Sede, Driade, Flexform, Flou, Poliform, Kartell,Ligne Roset, Living Divani, Porro and Vitra.

Habitat's highly trained, knowledgeable staff knows how to make modern design accessible and approachable. Working with their clientele, they help them choose items and customize interiors to reflect their lifestyle and needs. For those whose needs include a passionate expression of style, Habitat is an essential destination.

Hotel

Art+ Hotel

35 Ben Yehuda St.
Tel. (03) 542 5555
www.atlas.co.il

[Map 21]

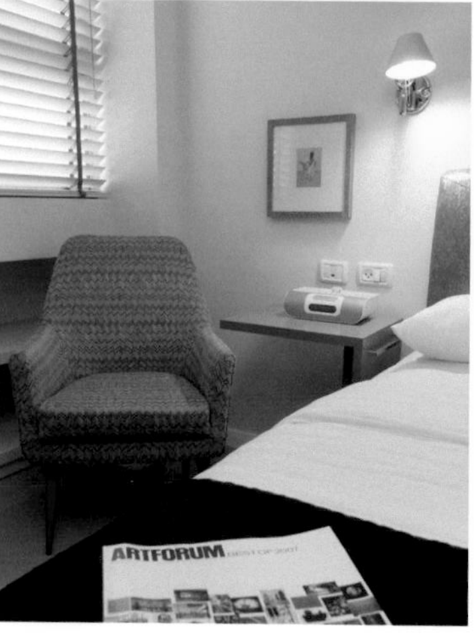

Located just steps from the beach, this brand-new, 62-room boutique hotel is dedicated to Israeli art. Five local artists were commissioned to create the murals that distinguish the décor on each floor; and meanwhile, video art by internationally famous Israeli artists is screened in the lobby. Retro style furniture has been combined with the clean lines of modern industrial design to create a cutting-edge atmosphere that highlights the Israeli art experience. Breakfast is served in the library, amongst books and magazines about – what else? – art.

Hotel

Center Hotel

[Map 22]

2 Zamenhoff St., Dizengoff Square
Tel. (03) 526 6100
www.atlas.co.il

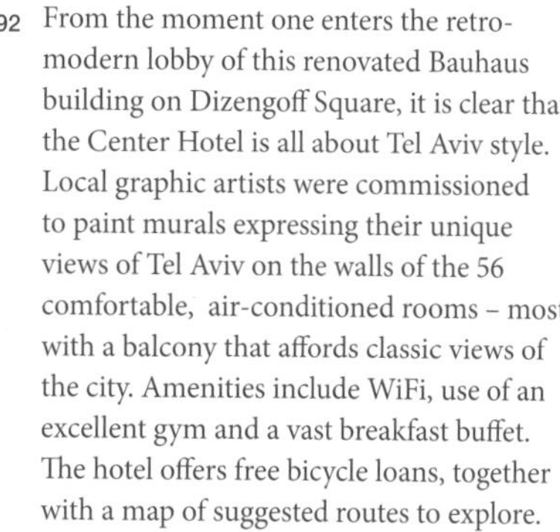

From the moment one enters the retro-modern lobby of this renovated Bauhaus building on Dizengoff Square, it is clear that the Center Hotel is all about Tel Aviv style. Local graphic artists were commissioned to paint murals expressing their unique views of Tel Aviv on the walls of the 56 comfortable, air-conditioned rooms – most with a balcony that affords classic views of the city. Amenities include WiFi, use of an excellent gym and a vast breakfast buffet. The hotel offers free bicycle loans, together with a map of suggested routes to explore.

Hotel

Cinema Hotel

1 Zamenhoff St., Dizengoff Square
Tel. (03) 520 7100
www.atlas.co.il

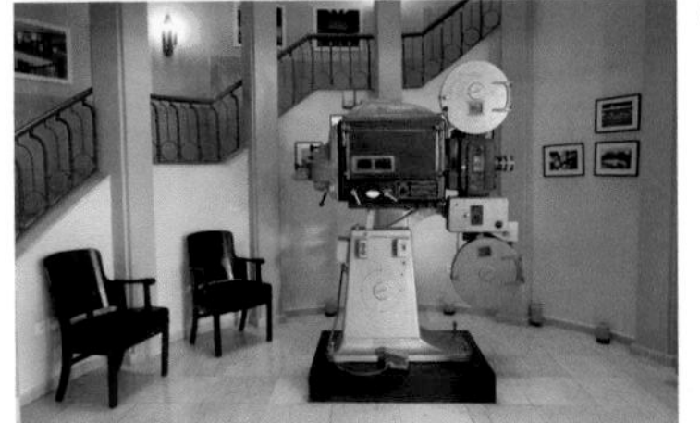

As its name suggests, this landmark Bauhaus structure was once one of the city's first cinemas. Now fully renovated, the Cinema Hotel is a charming boutique hotel in a prime location – right in the middle of the main shopping, eating and entertainment areas and within easy walking distance of the beach. The comfortably appointed, spotlessly clean rooms are air-conditioned and include free WiFi, satellite television, a private phone line with voice mail and a safe. Amongst the additional amenities are an extensive breakfast buffet, an enormous sun deck on the roof - which offers a classic view of Tel Aviv's rooftops - and use of a nearby health club. Movies are screened in the art deco lobby, and free popcorn is available from the remarkably friendly staff.

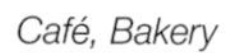

Café, Bakery

Bakery

72 Ibn Gvirol St.
Tel. (03) 696 1050

The Bakery's reputation for perfection preceded the opening of its Ibn Gvirol branch. For years the residents, fashionable shoppers and office workers who spend so much of their time walking along this lively stretch of central Tel Aviv's main thoroughfare had been forced to travel to Yad Harutzim in order to enjoy The Bakery's famous brioches, flaky croissants, golden muffins, tartes tatins, cakes, cookies and irresistible breads. The pleasure of a morning espresso and a better-than-Paris pain au chocolat consumed at a little marble-topped table was a privilege reserved for the lucky few who lived or worked in the area.
No wonder, then, that The Bakery on Ibn Gvirol became an instant hit. The espresso machine hisses non-stop during the early morning hours, before the start of the workday, as lawyers, judges, journalists and business owners line up for a pre-work cappuccino and pastry. Throughout the day, regular patrons who live in the area stop by for their regular Bakery goodness.

[Map 24]

More of the Best

Food

Amore Mio

100 Ibn Gvirol St.
Tel. (03) 524 4040

Italian Jewish immigrants serve home-style food prepared with the same warmth and care that they show their customers.

Ice cream

Amoretto

21 Ibn Gvirol St.
Tel. (03) 525 0602

This veteran Sicilian ice cream shop is a local legend. New flavors are introduced regularly, which is why a lot of regulars are true addicts.

Night

Armadillo Cerveza

174 Dizengoff St.
Tel. (03) 529 3277

This fabulous neighborhood bar is the sister of the original Armadillo on Ahad Ha'am Street. It offers a hip vibe, excellent homemade Middle Eastern bar food and a wide assortment of beers on tap.

Night

Averbuch

2 Reines St.
Tel. (03) 523 7719

Three former air force pilots wanted a place to entertain their friends, so they decided to open a bar. And then their friends' friends decided they liked it, too.

Café

Bacho

85 King George St.
Tel. (03) 528 9753

The hip and the trendy have gathered for years at this tiny neighborhood café. They come to lounge on the flea market furniture, enjoy impeccable coffee and homemade Italian ice cream, and check each other out.

Yoga

Bikram Yoga

14 Carlebach St.
Tel. (03) 624 1807

The local branch of the internationally famous "hot yoga" introduced by yoga guru Bikram Choudhury.

Books & Café

Bookworm

9 Malchei Israel St.
Tel. (03) 529 8490
www.bookworm.co.il

This cozy bookstore and café is a civilized Tel Aviv institution that provides food for the mind and body.

Night

Bukovsky

39 Frishman St.
Tel. (03) 523 2323

Named for author Charles Bukovsky, it started out as a simple neighborhood bar and went on to become one of the city's hippest late-night hangouts. Excellent DJs bring out the groove after midnight.

Hotel

Dan Tel Aviv

99 Hayarkon St.
Tel. (03) 520 2525
www.danhotels.co.il

Freshly renovated, this five-star hotel is considered one of Tel Aviv's top choices for luxury accommodation.

Children

Diada

75 Ben Gurion Blvd.
Tel. (03) 524 4484

This fabulous baby and parent center offers childcare, jamborees and a café for an all day experience that toddlers and caregivers alike will enjoy.

Food

Dixie Grill Bar

120 Yigal Alon St.
Tel. (03) 696 6123

Dixie was the first 24-hour restaurant in Tel Aviv. More than a decade later, it is still a popular stop for a late-night burger or post-clubbing steak.

Children's books

Emily

59 Ben Gurion Blvd.
Tel. (03) 523 9624

A charming children's bookshop that will enchant adults, too.

Food

Giraffe

49 Ibn Gvirol St.
Tel. (03) 691 6294

Giraffe is a trendy New York-style noodle bar that serves up generous portions of fresh and tasty Asian fusion food in a sleek, modern setting.

Night

Hamara

87 Hayarkon St.
Tel. (03) 522 6464

Located behind Rafael Restaurant, Hamara attracts an upscale crowd of sophisticated drinkers.

Food

Hinawi

25 Carlebach St.
Tel. (03) 624 0458

Wine and delicatessen.

Ice cream

Iceberg

108 Ben Yehuda St.
Tel. (03) 522 5025

Straight from Sicily, Iceberg is widely considered the very best Italian ice cream in Tel Aviv.

Fashion

Ido Recanati

13 Malchei Israel St., Rabin Square
Tel. (03) 529 8481

Originally from Spain, this widely-acclaimed designer creates collections of comfortable women's separates in bold colors and geometric shapes.

Food

Il Pastio

27 Ibn Gvirol St.
Tel. (03) 525 1166

This popular lunch spot serves fresh, homemade pasta and pizza in a pleasant setting.

Fashion

Katomenta

173 Dizengoff St.
Tel. (03) 527 9899
www.katomenta.com

Katomenta is a concept boutique that offers an innovative, alternative approach to fashion that has captured the attention of the local celebrity crowd.

Night, Food

La La Land

Gordon Beach
Tel. (03) 529 3303

This beach-front bar and restaurant is indisputably more sophisticated than any of the other greasy falafel spoons that line the Tel Aviv beachfront. The truth is that that's not saying too much, but La La Land is an attractive place to enjoy light finger food and drinks in summer and winter.

Café

Libra

120 Ben Yehuda St.
Tel. (03) 529 8764

The proprietor of this lovely, upscale café with the pleasant outdoor seating area is Mika Sharon, who has been a trend-setter in the Tel Aviv restaurant scene for more than a decade.

Food

Lilit

2 Dafna St.
Tel. (03) 609 1331

Lilit was the first gourmet kosher restaurant to open its doors in Tel Aviv. The culinary standards are very high and the décor is suitably elegant, making Lilit a popular choice for business lunches. Lilit also sets its own social agenda by hiring and training inner city youth.

Café

Lilush

73 Frishman St.
Tel. (03) 537 9354

This charming neighborhood café is famous for its panini.

Books, Café

The Little Prince

3 Simta Plonit St.
Tel. (03) 629 9387

Young poets and budding intellectuals gather at this cozy bookshop to read their works to one another and to discuss the latest developments in the Israeli literary scene.

Café

Masaryk Café

12 Masaryk Square
Tel. (03) 527 2411

Perched on a charming corner of Masaryk Square, this cosy, intimate café has for years been a favorite neighborhood hangout. It's a great place to start the day with a coffee and croissant.

Food

Meat Bar

52 Chen Blvd.
Tel. (03) 695 6276

This veteran steak bar is as popular today as it was the first year it opened, when it became an instant hit.

Jewelry

Miller

157 Dizengoff St.
Tel. (03) 524 9383

Miller is a high quality Israeli brand name that evokes quiet elegance in jewelry design

Night

Molly Bloom's

2 Mendele St.
Tel. (03) 522 1558

Molly Bloom's is a classic Irish pub that is particularly popular with ex-pats and diplomatic staff, who like to gather here to watch rugby and football games on the enormous screens while drinking a Guinness. There are also regular performances of live Irish music.

Food

Moon

58 Bograshov St.
Tel. (03) 629 1155

The conveyor belt sushi is straight out of downtown Tokyo at this fashionable Japanese eatery.

Food

Onami

18 Haarba'a St.
Tel. (03) 562 1172

For years, Onami has maintained its position as one of Tel Aviv's most popular Japanese restaurants.

Books

Pollak

36 King George St.
Tel. (03) 528 8613

Pollak's is a veteran second hand bookshop with an erudite staff and a pleasantly dusty atmosphere.

Shoes

Precious

63 Frishman St.
Tel. (03) 529 3814

The shoes sold at this brand-new shop include the trendiest names in footwear - e.g., Fly London and Fornarina.

Food

Raphael

87 Hayarkon St.
Tel. (03) 522 6464

Chef Rafi Cohen has earned critics' plaudits for his inventive Moroccan-French cuisine.

Fashion

Ronen Chen

155 Dizengoff St.
Tel. (03) 527 5672

With several branches in the greater Tel Aviv area, Canada and Western Europe, Ronen Chen is rapidly becoming a mini-empire with his clean-lined, simple but elegant casual separates for women.

Food

Sakura

79 King George St.
Tel. (03) 621 2900

Having established its reputation in Jerusalem, this popular Japanese restaurant opened a branch in Tel Aviv.

Design

Salon Saloma

25 Gordon St.
Tel. (03) 527 4150

It looks like your grandmother's living room, but Salon Saloma is in fact one of the city's most charming second hand shops. Everything on display is for sale.

Food

Shibuya

28 Bograshov St.
Tel. (03) 620 4927

Named for the busiest and chicest area of Tokyo, this fashionable Japanese restaurant is widely considered one of the best in the city.

Shoes

Shufra

108 Dizengoff St.
Tel. (03) 524 7274

This super-trendy casual shoe shop always has an eye-catching window display.

Night

Silon

89 King George St.
Tel. (03) 620 0053

Still one of the best, Silon pioneered the neighborhood bar concept in Tel Aviv.

Books

Steimatzky

109 Dizengoff St.
Tel. (03) 522 1513
www.steimatzky.co.il

Steimatzky is Israel's biggest national book chain. With several branches throughout the city, it is a convenient one-stop destination for those seeking popular English language books and periodicals.

Food

Tapeo

16 Haarba'a St.
Tel. (03) 624 0484

Spanish-style tapas customized for the Israeli palate are served in a sexy, sociable and dynamic atmosphere that is totally Tel Aviv.

Ice cream

Tel Hanan Ice Cream

68 King George St.

Tel Hanan opened its Tel Aviv branch after establishing its reputation in the Galilee region. This is a charming local ice cream joint that never fails to please.

Food

Thai House

8 Bograshov St.
Tel. (03) 517 8568

This is simply the best Thai restaurant in Israel. 'Nuff said.

DVD & Music

The Third Ear

48 King George St.
Tel. (03) 621 5200

For years, The Third Ear has sat at the top of the hill, as the best music shop and DVD library in Tel Aviv. The indisputably knowledgeable staff can come across as a bit grumpy sometimes, but don't take that personally. They're just very serious. Very!

Night

Toma

26 Ibn Gvirol St., ZOA House
Tel. (03) 695 6804

This enclosed outdoor bar is open from May to October, when it reigns supreme as the most pleasant al fresco watering hole in the city. The bar tenders are gorgeous, as are the women perched in front of them, and the atmosphere is sexy in typically Tel Aviv style.

Books

Tzomet Sfarim / Proza

163 Dizengoff St.
Tel. (03) 523 5477
www.booknetshop.co.il

Proza started as an independent bookshop and was recently purchased by Tzomet Sfarim, Israel's second largest bookshop chain. It retains its independent atmosphere, though. The staff is unusually knowledgeable and helpful, and the range of titles in Hebrew, English and French includes some excellent art and design books.

Food

Zepra

96 Yigal Alon St.
Tel. (03) 624 0044

Renowned for its ultra-modern décor, Zepra serves fashionable pan-Asian fusion cuisine that has garnered excellent reviews.

The Heart

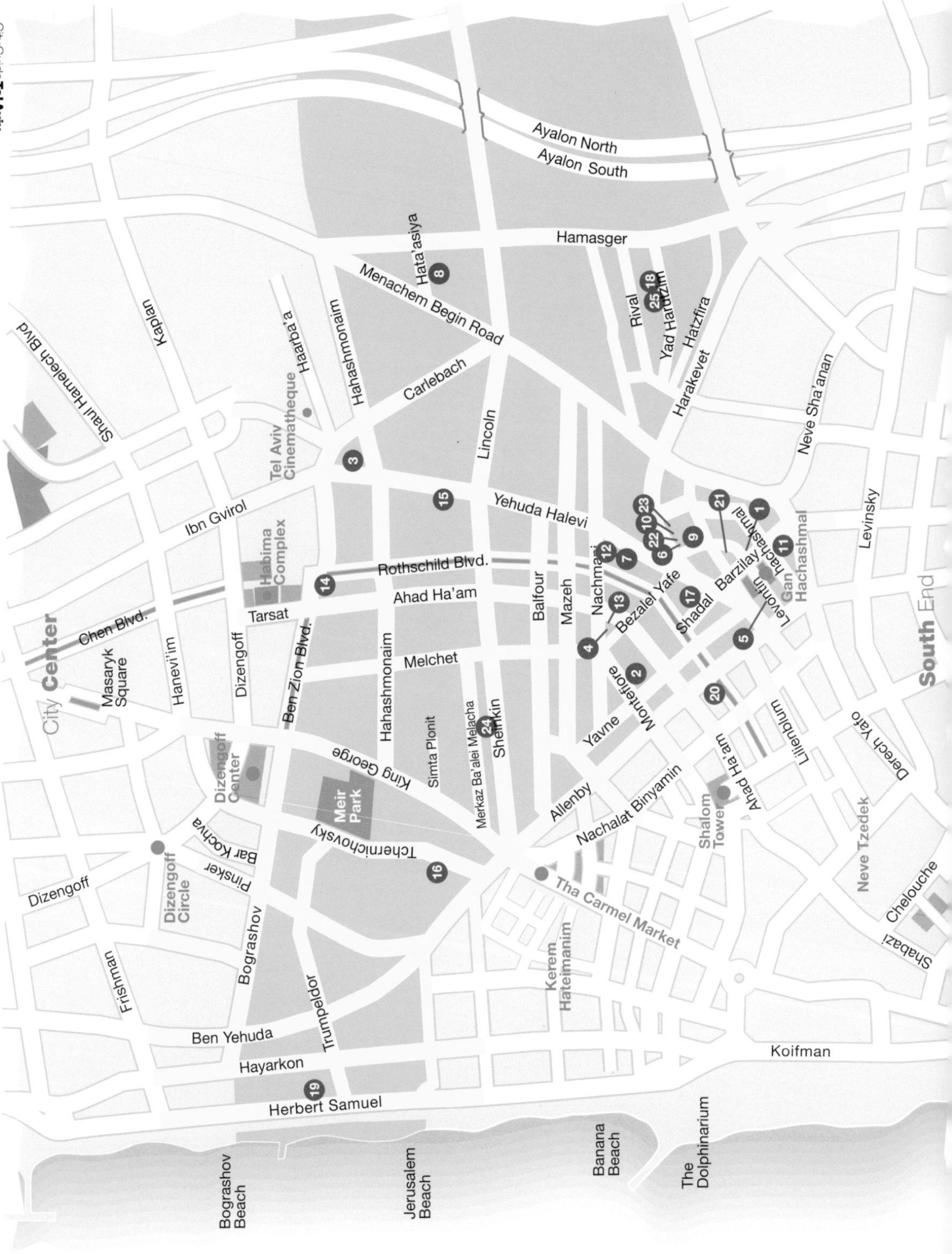

Ayalon North
Ayalon South
Hamasger
Hata'asiya
8
Menachem Begin Road
Rival
25 18
Yad Harutzim
Hatzfira
Harakevet
Neve Sha'anan
Kaplan
Shaul Hamelech Blvd
Haarba'a
Hahashmonaim
Carlebach
Tel Aviv Cinematheque
Lincoln
3
15
Yehuda Halevi
Ibn Gvirol
Habima Complex
Rothschild Blvd.
14
Ahad Ha'am
Tarsat
23
10
22
6
9
21
1
hachashmal
11
12
7
Nachmani
Barzilay
Levontin
Gan Hachashmal
Levinsky
South End
Bezalel Yafe
13
17
Shadal
5
4
Mazeh
Balfour
City Center
Chen Blvd.
Masaryk Square
Hanevi'im
Dizengoff
Ben Zion Blvd.
Hahashmonaim
Melchet
2
Montefiore
20
Yavne
Simta Plonit
Merkaz Ba'alei Melacha
24
Sheinkin
Lilienblum
Derech Yafo
King George
Dizengoff Center
Meir Park
Allenby
Nachalat Binyamin
Shalom Tower
Ahad Ha'am
Neve Tzedek
Bar Kochva
Tchernichovsky
Pinsker
Dizengoff
Dizengoff Circle
16
Tha Carmel Market
Chelouche
Shabazi
Bograshov
Kerem Hateimanim
Frishman
Trumpeldor
Ben Yehuda
Hayarkon
Koifman
19
Herbert Samuel
Bograshov Beach
Jerusalem Beach
Banana Beach
The Dolphinarium

The **Heart**

The area called the "heart" of Tel Aviv is one of the city's trendiest and most dynamic. Until recently it was an aging neighborhood, but over the past decade or so the heart has become the residence of choice for some of Israel's best known actors, writers, musicians and artists. This can make people watching particularly rewarding, especially at the local cafés.

The heart of the city is home to the Tel Aviv stock exchange, a branch of the Sotheby's auction house, investment banks, several prominent law firms and some of the city's most popular dining and nightlife spots. This diverse character drives the 24-hour atmosphere: No matter what the hour, there are almost always people on the streets in the heart of the city. The heart has something for nearly every visitor – amateur historians, shoppers with an eye for trendy local designers, art and culture enthusiasts, clubbers and gourmands. There are many young families living in the area, too, which gives it a real neighborhood feel.

Bordered on the north by Ben Zion Boulevard and on the south by Allenby Street, the heart of Tel Aviv is dominated by a tree-lined stretch of Rothschild Boulevard. Amongst the area's attractions are fashionable Sheinkin Street, many of the city's most popular restaurants, cafés and the hip and trendy Gan Hachashmal (Electricity Garden).

History

The heart of Tel Aviv is one of the city's oldest areas, dating back to the final years of the Ottoman era. Photographs taken of Rothschild Boulevard in the 1930s show symmetrical rows of shiny new Bauhaus-inspired, or International style, low-rise apartment building; these photos are the classic image of early Tel Aviv, but they do not show the area's earlier history. There is a relatively high concentration of old buildings in the pre-International eclectic style lining Allenby Street and dotting the side streets. Tel Aviv's first hotel and first brothel were both housed in eclectic style buildings located in the heart of the city. Today some of them have been restored, but most are in an appalling state of disrepair.

From the 1930s through the 1950s, when Allenby was a fashionable, boutique-and-café lined thoroughfare, the heart of the city was where the city's prosperous and stylish went to shop, socialize and stroll. But over the following two decades the area went into a period of decline. Tel Aviv experienced the same urban migration patterns as most Western cities, with the young and the prosperous moving to the northern suburbs and the new satellite towns beyond them. Business owners followed their customers, and Tel Aviv's formerly throbbing heart became an aging, neglected neighborhood.

Salvation came in the 1980s, when Tel Aviv's bohemians "discovered" the heart. Writers, actors and musicians moved into the neighborhood. They gathered in the trendy new cafés that opened on Sheinkin Street, which is how "Sheinkin type" came to be a catchall term that describes artsy-fartsy bleeding heart leftists. Edgy boutiques and shops opened up, and suddenly the heart of Tel Aviv was the coolest place to live.

The neighborhood's popularity increased rapidly over the following two decades, which naturally led to gentrification and an accompanying rise in real estate prices. Over the past 10 years, branches of chain stores have replaced Sheinkin's edgy little boutiques, while luxury apartment buildings have been built and many of the crumbling old International style buildings have been completely gutted and renovated to suit the taste and demands of discerning professional young urbanites.

But gentrification has not sterilized the heart - it remains a culturally and economically diverse neighborhood that is a remarkable island of tolerance in Israel's sharply divided society. Ultra-Orthodox Jews, high-tech millionaires, rock musicians, actors, leftist journalists, same sex couples, elderly veteran residents and artists live harmoniously on the same streets – often in the same building.

Rothschild Blvd.

Rothschild is easily the loveliest boulevard in Tel Aviv. It is certainly the most popular – especially along the section that is in the heart of the city. Shaded by ficus trees, lined with benches and dotted with outdoor coffee kiosks that sprang up over the last five years, Rothschild is one of the city's most charming

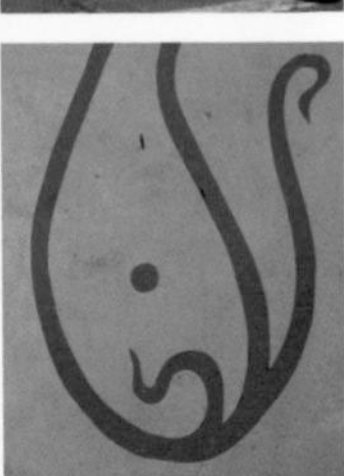

אהל מועד

places to stroll, bicycle and hang out. On weekends it is a magnet for suburbanites in search of a little Tel Aviv stardust: young families stroll, bike and stop for lunch at the cafés during the day; and club hoppers gather at one of the 24-hour restaurants or cafés after a night out. On weekdays, employees of the stock exchange, law offices and investment banks, with their slightly more formal attire, create a purposeful, downtown atmosphere.

But for all this activity, Rothschild still feels like it belongs to the people who live in the neighborhood. Locals gather on the boulevard for spontaneous games of petanques or chess on weekday evenings, and parents escorting their children to school gather at the boulevard kiosks for their morning coffee. On weekday afternoons, the benches are occupied by groups of the elderly, accompanied by their Philippine caregivers. And late on any given weekday night, twenty-something singletons who live in the neighborhood meet up with friends at the all-night café kiosks, which lately have also become casual, friendly pick-up spots.

The buildings lining Rothschild run the gamut of Tel Aviv styles, from Levantine eclectic to International, to sterile modern office towers. The latter are particularly prominent near Allenby Street, where developers have been given permission to build skyscrapers on condition that they also renovate a heritage building nearby.

There are several good restaurants along Rothschild and, of course, no shortage of cafés.

Yehuda Halevi St.

Yehuda Halevi is benefiting from gentrification. For decades it was just a noisy, unremarkable street that was a route to somewhere else, but over the past few years cafés, a trendy restaurant or two, some art galleries and upscale shops selling furniture and home accessories have moved in. It is too early to proclaim that Yehuda Halevi is the next cool street, but there are signs that it might be on its way – especially since the renovation and rehabilitation of Gan Hachashmal (Electricity Garden) was completed.

Gan Hachashmal

Gan Hachashmal, or Electricity Garden – so named because it was once the site of Tel Aviv's power plant – is indisputably the hippest place in the city to shop for original, cutting edge fashion by local designers.

If shopping is not your thing but music is, head over to Levontin 7. Named for its address, this small venue is the best music club in the city. The hippest, critically acclaimed up-and-coming musicians in jazz, hip hop, rock and indie, from all over the world perform here. There is a small bar upstairs, above the performance space. Performance dates and times are posted on the club's window, or you can check their website.

Yad Harutzim and **Hamasger** Sts.

The area around Yad Harutzim and Hamasger is a maze of auto repair shops, anodyne new office towers, traffic-clogged multi-lane roads and exhaust fumes. It is also Tel Aviv's newest up-and-coming commercial area.

Starting in 2000, Yad Harutzim became a sort of restaurant row, with several fashionable and well-reviewed eateries that made the street into a destination for local diners with discerning taste. Lately, however, Yad Harutzim has been looking a bit abandoned. Only one of the high-quality restaurant remains and, while it remains packed with customers at all hours, it is something of a rose in an otherwise neglected garden. This is probably a temporary situation. There are several well-trafficked small eateries, and a few clubs on the streets nearby, so the area is certainly busy. Tel Aviv is developing and evolving so rapidly that some entrepreneurial restaurateurs are bound to establish new places in this expanding business district.

Shadal St.

Tucked between shiny new office towers and renovated heritage houses is a beautiful old Sephardic synagogue that has been in constant use since it was established in 1928. This architecturally distinguished place of worship is particularly famous for its domed roof, and for the fact that it was the favored synagogue of the elite of the Sephardic community. Today it is a popular venue for weddings and circumcision ceremonies. The synagogue is open daily for visitors, and well worth a visit.

בית דינה שושנה גולדברג
D.SH.GOLDBERG

Coming
Soon

Ahad Ha'am St.

Named after Asher Ginzburg, a Tolstoyan philosopher of modern cultural Zionism and a Hebrew essayist whose pen name was Ahad Ha'am (One of the People), Ahad Ha'am is one of the most architecturally eclectic and historically interesting streets in Tel Aviv. It is also one of the longest, extending from Neve Tzedek all the way to Ben Zion Boulevard.

Montefiore St. and **Albert** Square

Perpendicular to Ahad Ha'am, Montefiore has some of the loveliest old structures in Tel Aviv – many of which have been lovingly restored over the past five years. Prince Albert Square, named after one of King George V's sons, is one of the most magical spots in Tel Aviv. A quirky little traffic island, with a tree-shaded bench shaded by an enormous ficus tree, it marks the point where Melchett, Nachmani and Montefiore Streets converge.

The striking Pagoda House dominates the square. Originally built as a hotel, the Pagoda House was for years an abandoned, decaying white elephant. Around the turn of this century, it was purchased by a private individual, completely renovated and turned into an impressively luxurious single-family home.

Sheinkin St.

Following a decline that began in the 1950s, when many residents moved to northern Tel Aviv, Sheinkin was "discovered" in the early 1980s by the bohemian café crowd. Over the following two decades Sheinkin became the heart of Israel's leftist-artist scene. Sheinkin was, and to many still is, the place for actors, musicians, writers and all those who like to be associated with them, to see and be seen. The street's name is also sometimes used to express derision: "Sheinkin types," pronounced with a sneer in one's voice, means "artsy fartsy bleeding heart leftists."

Over the past decade, though, Sheinkin has lost its edge a bit. It is still one of the most popular and best-known streets in Israel but, like New York's SoHo and Greenwich Village, it has become a victim of its cachet. Rising rents have resulted in the replacement of several small businesses with branches of chain stores.

But some of the old cafés and shops remain - like Café Tamar, a proudly leftist hangout on the corner of Ahad Ha'am that is owned by Sarah, the ultimate tough-love Jewish mother who knows what's good for you better than you do. Café Tamar is furnished with Formica tables and decorated with political posters that tout pretty much every popular issue on the left of the Israeli political scene. During the chilly rainy season, a handwritten sign on the door assures comfort-seeking customers that yes, there is homemade chicken soup with matzoh balls.

Perhaps the most fascinating anomaly of life in the Sheinkin area is the very visible presence of a large Hasidic community. Modestly dressed, bewigged women and men in traditional black coats live quietly and in apparent harmony alongside the scantily clad, tattooed and pierced. The contrast between radical post-modern chic and determinedly atavistic is most striking on Fridays, the first day of the weekend. For the first half of the day, the street is packed with suburban teenagers and tourists who turn the street into a place of frenetic activity, until the cafés and businesses close at around 3 p.m. The secular go home, the street falls silent as twilight approaches, and then groups of black-clad Hasidic men appear suddenly, walking rapidly toward the synagogue in order to greet the Sabbath.

Bialik St. and **Trumpeldor** Cemetery

Bialik Street is small, but important. This lovely cul-de-sac is dominated by the original home of H.N. Bialik, Israel's poet laureate. The home was recently renovated and is now a museum that is often used as a performance space for live music and literary events. The nearby home of Reuven Rubin, one of Israel's most important artists is also a museum where his life is chronicled and major works exhibited. Most recently, Tel Aviv's first Bauhaus Museum was established on Bialik Street.

The Trumpeldor Cemetery is Tel Aviv's equivalent of the Pére Lachaise in Paris. This is where country's most famous authors, artists and philosophers were laid to rest; a stroll here is like walking through a time capsule. It is a special place.

Meir Park

Located between Bograshov and Allenby, with entrances on Tchernichovsky and King George Streets, is Gan Meir, or Meir Park. Named for Meir Dizengoff, the first mayor of Tel Aviv, the park is a circular oasis of bench-lined, tree-shaded paths, a fishpond, a recently refurbished playground and the most popular dog run in the city. Despite the proximity of two noisy thoroughfares, Gan Meir is remarkably quiet. You can even hear the birds chirping.

Simta Almonit

If you are looking for someplace special to have a light lunch or coffee and cake after visiting Meir Park, cross King George Street and walk up a bit until you arrive at Simta Almonit, or Anonymous Alley. Here, in this tiny, dead-end street, you will find Salon Mazal, where Tel Aviv's anarchist community has a bookshop and hosts various speakers and events; and next to Salon Mazal there is a little café with a charming, enclosed garden out back. If you feel like doing a little shopping, check out the boutique at the end of the alley. In keeping with the anarchist-activist spirit of Simta Almonit, it is called "Machteret," or Underground.

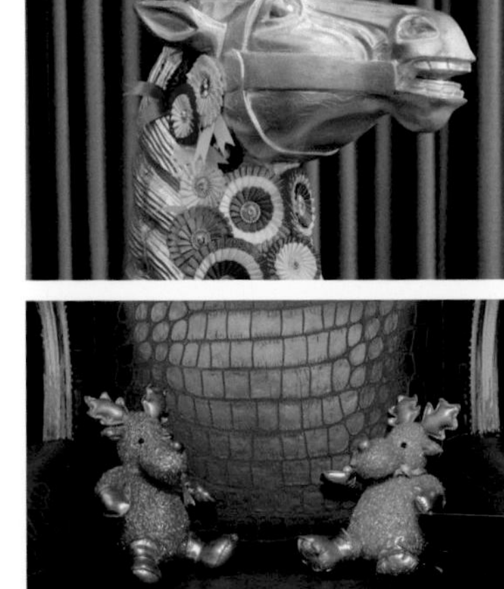

Fashion

Art-C-Ifrach

5 Barzilay St., Gan Hachashmal
Tel. (077) 553 3455
www.art-c-ifrach.com

Having gathered an international following of ardent admirers over the past decade, designer Artzi Ifrach recently opened his own shop in the cutting edge Gan Hachashmal area.

The street-level entrance, with its enormous Union Jack flag and larger-than-life sized mannequins draped in extraordinary, Sgt. Pepper-like outfits, looks like the foyer of a funky fashion museum – which is fitting, because the stunning collections in the boutique downstairs are pure art. No matter what your taste in fashion, it is impossible to remain indifferent to Artzi Ifrach's unique, frequently iconoclastic garments - which carry more than a passing reference to Vivienne Westwood and John Galliano. Refurbished and reworked vintage pieces hang next to original designs. Icons are deconstructed in playful, out-of-context interpretations that are an homage to the designer's love of objects and his fondness for breaking the rules. Each garment is a one-off creation that can be purchased off the rack or custom tailored, and Artzi designs an entire new collection every week. He also designs custom-made outfits, including unforgettable bridal gowns.

The vintage jewelry and accessories displayed in glass cases, or artfully scattered on shelves throughout the boutique, complete the impression of being in an extraordinary gallery dedicated to the art of fashion.

[Map 1]

Hotel

Hotel Montefiore

36 Montefiore St.
Tel. (03) 564 6100
www.hotelmontefiore.co.il

Hotel Montefiore is an oasis of style, service, intimacy and luxury that has no peer in Tel Aviv. Located on one of the most romantic streets in the heart of the city, just steps from Prince Albert Square, this meticulously restored, 1920s heritage building houses 12 elegantly appointed rooms, plus a hip restaurant and bar. From the very first glance, it is clear that every single detail of the décor and amenities have been considered. Hotel Montefiore is at the same standard as the very best luxury boutique hotels in London and New York. This attention to luxury, detail and comfort extends to the customized service. Each guest is assigned a staff member that can be contacted directly 24 hours a day to assist and provide every possible service the guest might need or want. The Montefiore offers services such as a picnic basket that contains a gourmet lunch, wine and suntan lotion for a day at the beach; difficult-to-obtain restaurant reservation and theater tickets; or a night on the town with an insider who acts as a guide to the best of the city's complex club scene.
Located on the main floor, the hotel's restaurant serves brasserie cuisine with Vietnamese influences. For the worldly traveler who expects the highest standards in luxury and service, but prefers the intimacy and charm of a boutique hotel to the cookie cutter ambiance of a chain hotel, the Montefiore is simply ideal.

DH
LAWRENCE
CHARLES FRAZIER
THE FREEDOM LINE
PETER
EISNER

[Map 2]

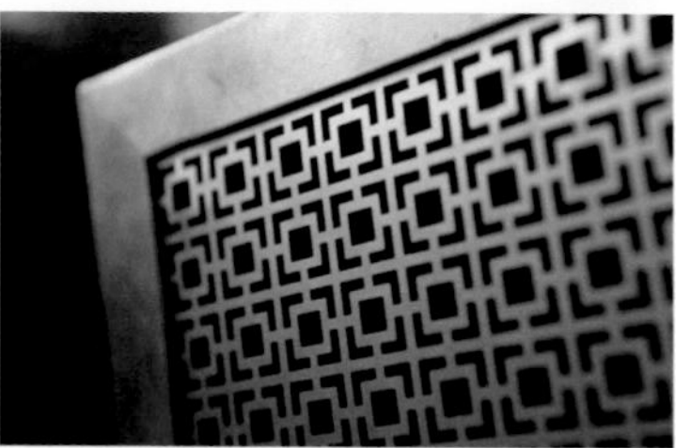

Design

Villa Maroc

110 Yehuda Halevi St.
Tel. (03) 562 0401
www.villamaroc.co.il

Famed design duo Dganit and Yossi Cohen have re-interpreted contemporary Moroccan design for the modern, high-tech, lived-in home. Together, they have corrected misconceptions about Moroccan and Middle Eastern ethnic style by demonstrating that it is truly contemporary – as shown in their Morrocan "villa," a showroom reached by a separate entrance behind the shop.

At Villa Maroc, customers choose from a stunning variety of imported Moroccan and Middle Eastern fabric, furniture, lighting solutions and home accessories in a delightfully warm, colorful and inviting environment. Together with their expertly trained staff, the Cohens show their customers how to realize their Middle Eastern dream homes, using the language of contemporary ethnic design. Consultations are free, and all customization work is done at the Villa Maroc factories in Israel.

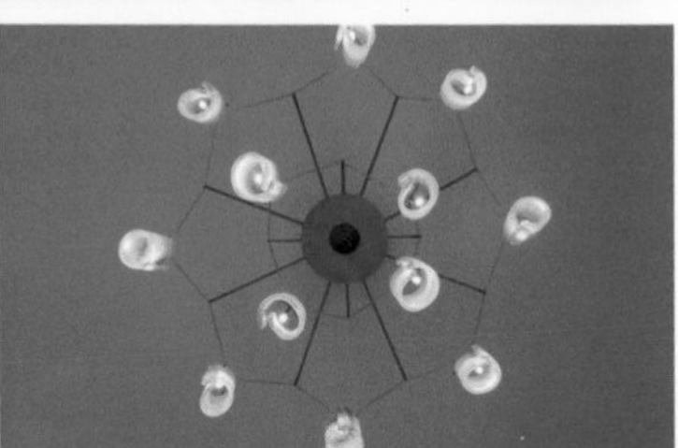

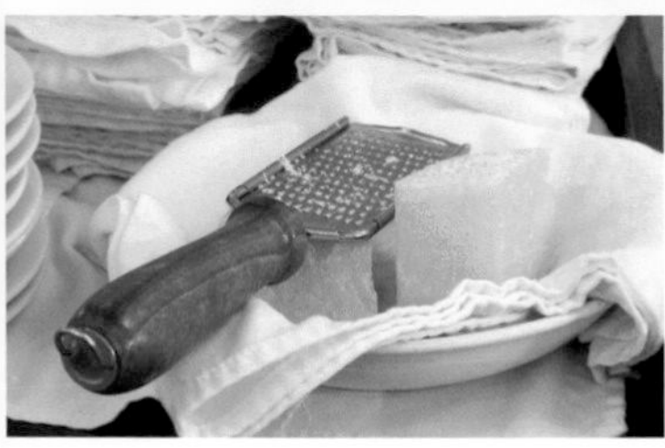

Food

Pronto

26 Nachmani St.
Tel. (03) 566 0915
www.pronto.co.il

This casually elegant restaurant has set the standard for Italian restaurants in Israel for nearly two decades. Pronto is a popular lunchtime venue for well-heeled business people and diplomats, and is invariably fully booked for dinner, with reserved parking a much-appreciated bonus. The uncomplicated menu offers familiar Italian fare that starts with antipasti and salads, and continues with pastas, risotto, meats and fish. The extensive wine list focuses on superior Italian vintages, many of which are stored on the floor-to-ceiling shelves. Owner Rafi Adar, who lived for nearly a decade in Rome, was awarded the Cavaliere della Repubblica Italiana for his contribution to promoting Italian cuisine abroad. The framed certificate is displayed discreetly, near the bar.

[Map 5]

Yoga

Yoga at Gan Hachashmal

9 Levontin St.
Tel. (03) 560 1225
www.goyoga.co.il

This spacious, light-filled yoga studio in the heart of Tel Aviv's trendiest district feels like a fabulous, cozy downtown loft apartment. The sense of "home" is intentional: Yoga at Gan Hachashmal consciously nurtures an intimate, warm atmosphere.
Similarly, the approach to ashtanga/vinyasa asana practice is friendly and non-dogmatic, catering to all levels with several classes daily. The knowledgeable instructors frequently and gently remind students to practice asanas carefully and avoid physical injury. After class, students and instructors linger in the reception-area-cum-living-room, chatting over cookies and herbal tea. One can also purchase mats and organic cotton yoga clothes at the yoga boutique. The studio holds regular workshops, often led by prominent international yoga gurus.

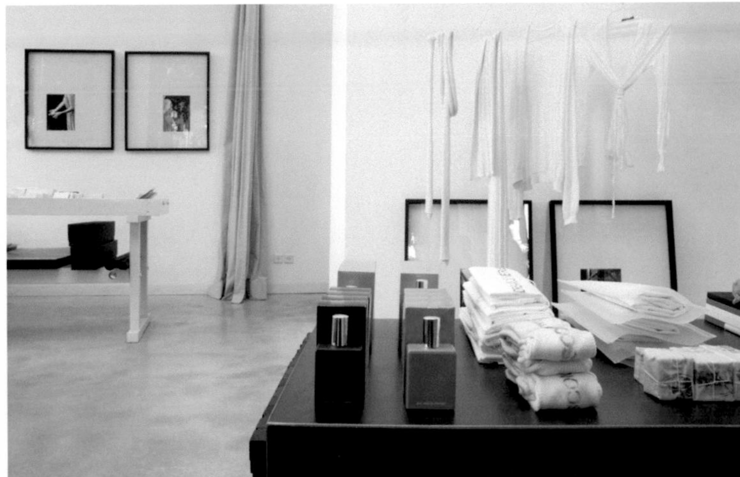

Fashion, Design

Sharon Brunsher

12 Harakevet St.
Tel. (03) 560 4834
www.brunsher.com

[Map 6]

With its elegant, monochromatic, industrial-architectural design, Sharon Brunsher looks as if it were transported from New York's fashionable SoHo district. In fact, the boutique and the owner/designer's collections are inspired by her love affair with Paris.

Sharon Brunsher combines contrasts to create a cohesive, aesthetically pleasing whole. White and black, smooth and textured, old and new, simplicity and complexity – all are essential elements of the designer's collections of clothes, bed linens, home accessories, jewelry and stationery. The garments of cotton and wool are constructed from the finest materials, to drape the body elegantly. The sheets are of pure Egyptian cotton, and the knitted blankets are softly luxurious. Ms. Brunsher designs her own line of notebooks, bound in both antique and modern covers. Taken as a whole, the objects and garments in this lovely boutique speak a single, harmonious language of design.

[Map 7]

Food

Arbinka

87 Yehuda Halevi St.
Tel. (03) 566 8777

Arbinka is a sophisticated Spanish-style restaurant and lounge bar that radiates a chic, sexy atmosphere. It attracts a worldly clientele who come to enjoy good company, hip, danceable electronic music and expertly prepared drinks. The drinks go particularly well with the chef's creative, Mediterranean-influenced tapas. The Spanish-style appetizers are available in vegetarian, seafood and meat options and are perfect bar food, making a delightful snack or light meal. The scene at Arbinka tends to be urbane and cosmopolitan, which is why it attracts a good-looking crowd that really knows how to enjoy life.

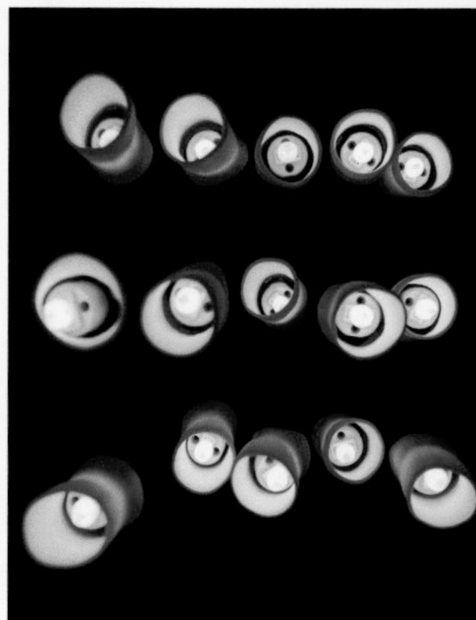

Deca

10 Hata'asiya St.
Tel. (03) 562 9900

Deca aspires successfully to redefine the Tel Aviv dining scene with its kosher contemporary gourmet Mediterranean cuisine. Inspired by familiar local flavours and prepared with great skill from the freshest, highest quality ingredients, the sun-and-sea kissed dishes emerging from Deca's kitchen have won excellent reviews from the city's toughest food critics. Chef Yaniv Caspi created the fish and dairy-based menu in consultation with celebrity Chef Haim Cohen, who has for years communicated his love for Levantine cooking via his popular weekly cooking show. Alon Baronovich, the highly regarded architect whose resume includes several of Tel Aviv's most prestigious restaurants, created for Deca a unique décor that successfully merges traditional, contemporary and industrial elements. The result is absolutely striking, and indisputably stylish.

[Map 8]

FRESH PRODUCTS SERVED DAILY

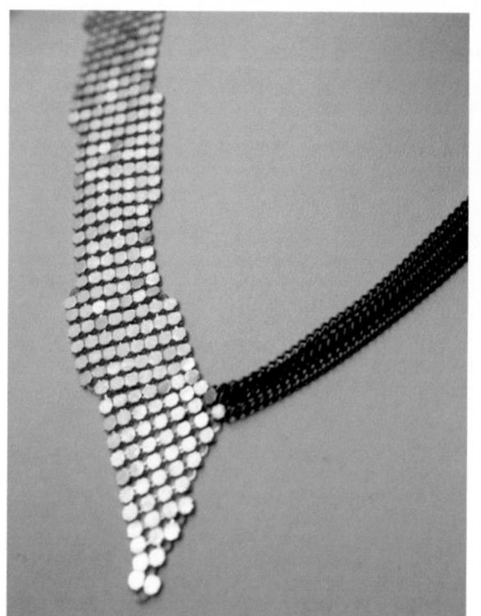

Design

Ruby Star

28 Levontin St.
Tel. (077) 560 6500
www.rubystar-accessories.com

It takes a few minutes to appreciate the full impact of Shirley Itzik's whimsical, stylish boutique. Taking her inspiration from street fashion and her own unique vision, the young designer creates fabulously sexy jewelry that is sensual and thought provoking, appealing equally to young hipsters and sophisticated jewelry lovers. Leather is combined with precious metal; religious icons are removed from their context and re-interpreted with a pop sensibility; discarded motor parts dangle from delicate leather straps; and semi-precious stones are set in stainless steel. Each object is made with painstaking attention to detail and imaginatively displayed. Itzik's own leather belts are arrayed alongside vintage shoes, Kung Fu sneakers and a line of imported avant-garde T-shirts.

Design

More Design

12 Harakevet St.
Tel. (03) 560 5297
(054) 667 7619

Designer Mor Bar-Menachem opened her studio shop in the fashionable Gan Hachashmal area after building her reputation as a leading designer of high-quality leather bags for some of the most exclusive boutiques in Israel. Focusing on clean lines, comfort and elegance, she uses the highest quality leathers to create bags that appeal to today's active women. The designer focuses her designs on highlighting the unique qualities of each piece of leather, creating a striking accessory that completes a woman's outfit with style and taste.

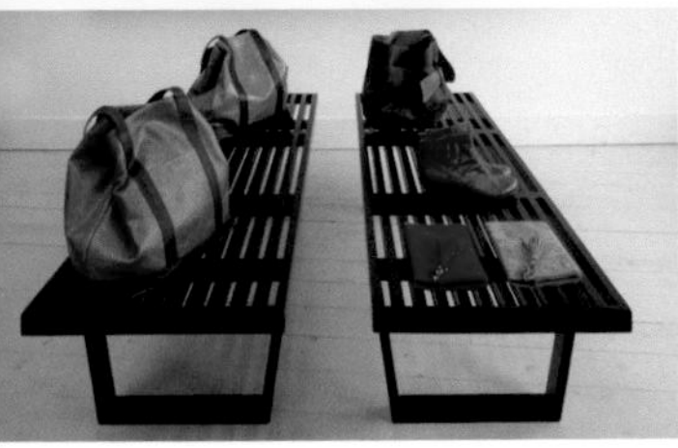

[Map 10]

Fashion

Nona Elga

12 Barzilay St.
Tel. (03) 560 1257

[Map 11]

Designer Limor Diana-Hasson creates fashion for women, not girls, and she possesses a deep understanding of what intelligent, active urban Israeli women want to wear. Feminine but practical, body conscious yet flattering, suitable for both day and evening, her clothes are made of natural fabrics like cotton, wool and viscose. They are well suited to the Israeli climate, although they certainly travel well, and reflect perfectly Tel Aviv's casual but fashion-conscious attitude. There is an undeniable intelligence in the designs, with romantic dresses showing retro influences and masculine trousers re-interpreted for the female form.

Design

Sarit Shani Hay

36 Nachmani St.
Tel. (03) 566 6987
www.shanihay.co.il

[Map 12]

Located in an old apartment building, designer Sarit Shani Hay's extraordinary showroom is characterized by her signature bold colors and unique interpretation of contemporary style for intimate spaces – particularly, but not exclusively, bedrooms for children and adults. The designer intentionally combines traditional and modern elements for an effect that is eclectic, and simultaneously warm and cold. Ms. Shani Hay also designs unique home decorating accessories, many of which are a reflection of the period she lived in Africa. Her anatomically correct monkey doll is particularly striking, appealing equally to both children and adults.
Above all, Sarit Shani Hay is meant to feel like a home, rather than an impersonal exhibition space. This is also the designer/artist's studio, where she creates customized furniture and interior design solutions for her clientele. All the work is done locally and by hand, in her own factory.

Food

Café Noir

43 Ahad Ha'am St.
Tel. (03) 566 3018

Café Noir has been an institution for more than a decade, but it remains as popular today as it was when it first opened. The secret to its success is simple, comfortable, old-fashioned décor, warm lighting, good service, a casual atmosphere and reliably good upscale comfort food.

Café Noir's signature dish is its schnitzel, which is widely considered the best in Israel. Choose a chicken, veal or pork cutlet that is pounded thin, breaded, crisply fried in classic Viennese style, and served with silky mashed potatoes. Recently, Café Noir's in-house pastry chef has introduced delectable homemade bread and classic desserts – such as the highly recommended tiramisu.

Café Noir has many regulars, from the breakfast crowd of journalists and politicians, through the business lunch bunch, to the late night bar crowd. No matter what the hour, the atmosphere is welcoming.

[Map 13]

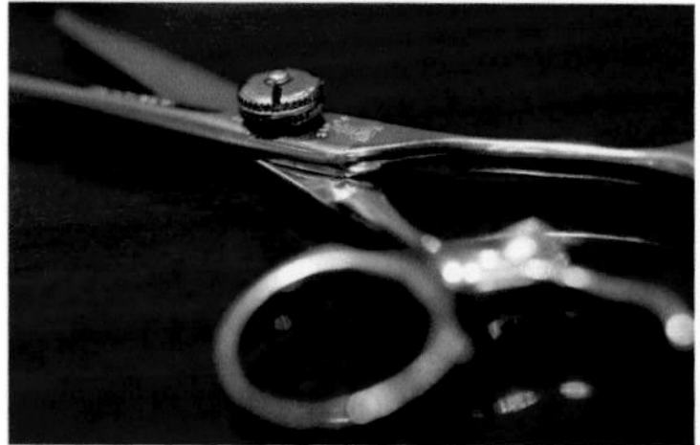

[Map 14]

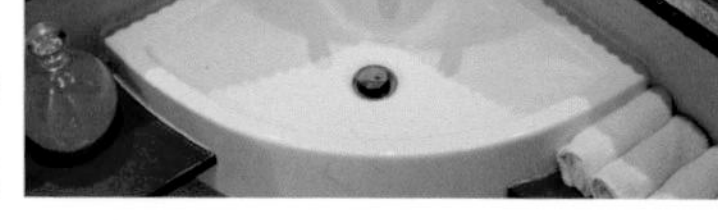

Hair design

Collie Hair Design

141 Rothschild Blvd.
Tel. (03) 685 2020
www.collie.co.il

Located in a landmark Bauhaus building opposite Habimah Theater, Collie is an intimate hair styling boutique that conveys an atmosphere of luxury, elegance and cutting-edge style. Collie is one of the country's most renowned hair artists. His reputation is based on a holistic approach to design and color, which is informed by the uncompromising philosophy that one's hair should be an expression of one's personal style, and that its shape must integrate seamlessly with the body and its movement. Collie and his talented staff provide each of their clients with the unforgettable experience of expert, personalized attention. In addition to cutting and color, Collie offers hair straightening using the Japanese technique, as well as a private room for bridal hair styling.

esign

etro-TLV

23 Yehuda Halevi St.
el. (03) 685 0663
www.retro-tlv.com

etro-TLV is a Mecca of mid-twentieth entury classic design. Original creations by cclaimed designers such as Charles & Ray ames, George Nelson and Joe Colombo nd leading manufacturers Fritz Hanssen, Iermann Miller, Knoll and Martinelli re expertly restored and displayed with npeccable contemporary chic style. While nost objects are from the retro-modern eriod, there are also many examples from ne Art Deco period and the 1970s. For ustomers seeking expert advice on how to ntegrate classic pieces in a contemporary nvironment, Retro-TLV offers customized esign consulting services.

[Map 15]

Books

SketchBook

5 Tchernichovsky St.
Tel. (03) 620 1351
www.sketchbook.co.il

[Map 16]

This bright, welcoming and aesthetically pleasing space houses Tel Aviv's widest and most up-to-date selection of quality books on design, art, architecture and fashion. Meir, Sketchbook's modest and friendly proprietor, is an enthusiastic fan of the dynamic Israeli design scene. Besides the books and the pleasing selection of high-end writing tools and accessories, he stocks quirky, charming and innovative creations by Israeli designers and graphic artists. He has also turned the upstairs area into a gallery, where works by recent art and design school graduates are shown in constantly changing exhibitions.

Night

Mental

7 Shadal St.
Tel. (03) 560 5655

[Map 17]

Welcome to one of the hippest hangouts in Tel Aviv – where the beautiful people, buzzing bar and cutting-edge music combine to create an edgy, sexy energy that seduces and doesn't let go. Named Bar of the Year (2007) by Time Out Tel Aviv, Mental hosts a late-night scene that starts at midnight and frequently continues past dawn. The superior sound system amplifies progressive-electronic sounds spun by a very impressive line-up of DJ's - including the best-known names of both the Israeli and European club circuit. Well-known groups perform live on Monday nights, inevitably raising the energy to peak levels for an appreciative audience. And Ridiculous Tuesdays must be experienced to be understood (you won't be disappointed).

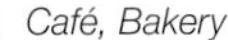

Café, Bakery

Bakery

13 Yad Harutzim St.
Tel. (03) 537 1041

The hand of perfection is apparent in every detail of The Bakery's décor, service, pastries, breads and cakes. There are many excellent patisseries and upscale bread shops in Tel Aviv, but in the end they are all nipping at the heels of The Bakery, which sails serenely ahead, secure in the knowledge that they know how to do things the way they are supposed to be done. Berry-filled pastries, flaky croissants, golden muffins, tartes tatins, yeast cakes and buttery cookies seduce the eye, while the primordial odor of baking bread conquers the olfactory sense. Baguettes, whole wheat, white and sourdough breads are piled neatly on the dark wooden shelves, which complement the traditional marble counters and stainless steel accessories to create a pleasing, retro-modern effect. There are three small, marble topped tables at the entrance, where a perfect espresso can be enjoyed together with a morning pastry or an afternoon sandwich.

[Map 18]

Hotel

Sea Executive Suites

76 Herbert Samuel St.
Tel. (03) 795 3434
www.sea-hotel.co.il

This stylish boutique hotel facing the beach provides delightful accommodation for business travellers and tourists alike. Each well-appointed suite includes a mini-office with free ADSL connection, computer, fax, private email address and phone line. Additional amenities include a fully equipped kitchenette and a home movie system with 29-inch television and DVD, with a DVD library in the lobby. There is a 24-hour gym and a dry sauna on the premises, plus convenient maid and laundry service. The extensive continental breakfast buffet is served in the dining area, while take-away meals can be ordered for lunch and dinner from any of the nearby restaurants, via the courteous staff at the front desk. Espresso and homemade cookies are served daily in the elegant lobby, which faces the beach. At dusk the lights are dimmed and soft music plays, creating an intimate atmosphere.

Food

Benedict Blvd.

29 Rothschild Blvd., corner of Allenby St.
Tel. (03) 686 8657

Expanding upon the success of the original Benedict on Ben Yehuda Street, Benedict Boulevard brings its fabulous 24-hour breakfast concept to the heart of Tel Aviv, right at the point where the city's legendary nightlife meets its dynamic commercial center. In other words, do expect to see clubbers ending a late night over an English breakfast, alongside bankers beginning their day over the same meal. While the menu here includes some creative new dishes, including charcuterie and beef additions, and there is a flagstone patio for breakfast al fresco, the owners have wisely maintained the winning Benedict formula - it's all about breakfast - that made the original a critical and popular success.

[Map 20]

Design

Mishi

17A Levontin St.
Tel. (077) 787 8729
www.mishi-design.com

Meirav Ohayon refers to her boutique, located in an airy, early twentieth century pre-Bauhaus ground-floor apartment, as her "laboratory." This is where she designs and sells her line of unique fabric and leather bags, wallets and accessories. Her artistic and design philosophy are reflected in the clean lines, body-consciousness and comfort that characterize the constantly evolving collection of day and evening bags. The sophisticated merging of comfort and style appeals to a wide range of tastes. Thoughtful and endearing touches include hidden pockets in all the bags.

[Map 21]

[Map 22]

Fashion

Closet Collection

12 Harakevet St.
Tel. (03) 560 2571

With her collections of classic separates and dresses, designer Mirit Rodrig successfully fulfills her goal of providing a complete wardrobe for all occasions in one location. Essential elements of Ms. Rodrig's fashion sensibility include hand-embroidered details, shawls, scarves and a variety of colors which, taken as a whole, present a cohesive look that each client can interpret according to her own personality. The designer purposely creates high-quality, classic garments that are timeless and suitable for daywear, eveningwear and all the important events in a busy, intelligent woman's life.

Design

Paula Bianco

2 Harakevet St.
Tel. (03) 685 0171
www.paulabianco.biz

[Map 23]

Taking her inspiration from unusual materials that range from climbing rope to art deco crystals, designer Smadar Pola Azriel creates complex jewelry that is feminine, sophisticated, indisputably unique and completely ageless. With a background that includes more than three years as a designer at Kastiel Furniture, Smadar's deep understanding of precise, high quality workmanship and aesthetics is evident in each piece. This knowledge extends to the décor of her boutique, with its strong sense of history of place and dominant wood accents that evoke a sense of tradition combined with contemporary creativity.

Food

Orna and Ella

33 Sheinkin St.
Tel. (03) 620 4753

[Map 24]

Orna and Ella is a Tel Aviv icon so famous that it has entered the national lexicon of cultural references. For many, this 14-year-old café and restaurant is the only truly important reason to visit Sheinkin Street. Orna and Ella, the names behind the legend, nurtured what began as a tiny café into a restaurant that serves a varied menu of mostly Italian and French-influenced cuisine. Everything, including the bread, is lovingly prepared on the premises. The serving staff is equally famous for their professionalism and their good looks.

[Map 25]

Food

Coffee Bar

13 Yad Harutzim St.
Tel. (03) 688 9696

The Coffee Bar is the quintessential familiar bistro. It is also a Tel Aviv institution. With its lively atmosphere, efficient, friendly service and casually elegant décor, the Coffee Bar was a maverick when it opened its doors 15 years ago in the grungy industrial area of Yad Harutzim. Its trendy, stylish fare pioneered the Tel Aviv bistro scene in particular, and the city's culinary renaissance of the mid-1990's in general. But while there are many imitators, there is only one Coffee Bar. More than a decade after it became an instant success, it remains one of the city's best restaurants - a metaphor for longevity and excellence. From early morning until late at night, the Coffee Bar hums with energy. Early morning patrons enjoy breakfast accompanied by classical music, while the power-lunch crowd creates a purposeful atmosphere. Throughout the week, regular patrons from all over Greater Tel Aviv flock to the Coffee Bar for dinner, where they indulge a shared fondness for upscale comfort food – such as sauteed chicken livers on silky mashed potatoes or a simple grilled Mediterranean fish. For those who prefer more sophisticated fare, the menu features bistro standards like confit de canard, seafood risotto, or a perfectly prepared steak served with bone marrow. Daily specials are hand written in chalk on the large blackboards.

More of the Best

Night

Academia

6 Montefiore St.

As far as mega-bars are concerned, Academia is the city's newest and hottest place to see and be seen.

Fashion

Alma

9 Merkaz Ba'alei Melacha St.
Tel. (03) 620 0145

For drop-dead chic local designs for women, stop by Alma. You won't leave empty handed.

Night

Armadillo

51 Ahad Ha'am St.
Tel. (03) 620 5573

Cozy and indisputably hip, Armadillo is the best kind of neighborhood bar. There is a wide range of beers on tap, and the homemade Levantine comfort food goes beautifully with a few drinks.

Night

Atara

32 Rothschild Blvd.

All the celebs are packing in to Atara. It's a hot bar with an excellent pick up scene for those who are in the mood for a sexy atmosphere.

Night

Barzilay

13 Harechev St.
Tel. (03) 687 8090
www.barzilayclub.com

The hottest live acts perform at Barzilay, where the atmosphere is supremely cool. This is an essential venue for anyone who wants to experience the rough edges of Tel Aviv's legendary night life.

Shoes

Behonot

11 Sheinkin St.
Tel. (03) 620 9295

One of the funkiest shoe shops on Sheinkin Street, where you can find all the latest imported trends.

Food

Beta Pizza

Hillel Hazaken St.
corner of Hacarmel Market
Tel. (1599) 509 090

If Italian tourists go to Beta for their pizza fix, you know it must be the best in town. The thin crusts and gourmet toppings are irresistible, and there are salads and pasta dishes as well. This new branch saves you the time to go all the way up north to the port.

Night

Breakfast Club

6 Rothschild Blvd.

Tucked away at the foot of Rothschild Boulevard, the Breakfast Club is still one of the coolest late-late night spots in the city. It opens at midnight, but only starts to warm up after 2 a.m.

Café

Café Ben Ami

22 Nachmani St., Albert Square
Tel. (03) 560 9960

The pastries at this elegant coffee shop and patisserie run the gamut from central European chocolate babkas to sophisticated, dense chocolate cakes that would make the best French and Viennese pastry shops proud. Everything is reliably delicious, and clearly prepared with the highest quality ingredients. There is a charming outdoor seating area, where one can enjoy cake and coffee while looking out over romantic Albert Square.

Café

Café Noah

91 Ahad Ha'am St.
Tel. (03) 629 3799

Regularly voted one of the city's top 10 cafés, this neighborhood hangout is a charming, cozy place to enjoy a meal or coffee with friends, or to sit and work on one's laptop. The café hosts live music on Sunday nights.

Café

Café Tamar

57 Sheinkin St.
Tel. (03) 685 2376

There's no décor and the food is forgettable, but Café Tamar is a legend. It was once the beating heart of Tel Aviv's intellectual bohemian scene, and still hosts a sort of "parliament" of veterans on Friday afternoons, but otherwise its place has been usurped by nearby cafés like Noach, Ginzburg and Orna and Ella. Still, it's definitely worth a stop – especially in the winter, when owner Sarah Stern serves up her homemade chicken soup.

Food

Cantina

71 Rothschild Blvd.
Tel. (03) 620 5051

All the celebs eat at Cantina. The food is good, although the service is a little chilly sometimes, but if you are looking for the ultimate people watching experience, head to Cantina for lunch. Don't be surprised if you see the local paparazzi lurking around.

Design

Carousella

27 Rothschild Blvd.
Tel. (03) 560 3750

For charming, tasteful and (let's face it) expensive furnishings and accessories for children's bedrooms, you will find everything you're looking for at Carousella.

Café

Confiserie

4 Tchernichovsky St.
Tel. (03) 620 3022
www.confiserie.co.il

The homemade pastries at Confiserie are only one reason to stop by. This charming café is always packed with artistic-looking, beautiful people and the décor is cozy and contemporary.

Fashion

Delicatessen

4 Barzilay St.
Tel. (03) 560 2297

Designer Idit Barak has earned international acclaim in important international fashion publications for her playful, individual and sophisticated designs.

Fashion

Dina Glass

35 Nachmani St.
Tel. (03) 560 2493

This gem of a tiny boutique is where designer Dina Glass creates her feminine, chic and unique collections for women.

Design

Elemento

119 Rothschild Blvd.
Tel. (03) 620 9848

Tucked inside an unprepossessing pre-Bauhaus building, Elemento is a very pleasant surprise. The owners import chic contemporary and retro furniture and home accessories, which they display with impeccable taste.

Night

Evita

31 Yavneh St.
Tel. (03) 566 9559

It might come as a surprise to discover that Tel Aviv has only one gay bar, but the fact is that this city is so gay-friendly that there's really no need for them to segregate themselves. This is why Evita, although nominally a gay bar, actually attracts a lot of heterosexual regulars who come just for the good vibe, good food and good music.

Fashion

Frau Blau

8 Hachashmal St.
Tel. (03) 560 1735

Fashion designer Helene Blaunstein and her partner Philip Blau create arresting, funky and absolutely unique designs.

Night

Gilda

64 Ahad Ha'am St.
Tel. (03) 560 3588

Gilda is a charming neighborhood bar that is open from the afternoon until late at night. The kubbeh soup is already famous.

Café

Ginzburg

55 Ahad Ha'am St.
Tel. (03) 560 8070

Regularly mentioned in all the lists of the city's top cafés, Ginzburg is an unpretentious neighborhood hangout that serves standard café food in a cozy, welcoming atmosphere. The coffee is excellent, and the homemade croissants, pain au chocolats and brioches are a local legend. Ginzburg attracts an intellectual, artsy crowd – including many famous writers and musicians.

Night

Jewish Princess

67 Yehuda Halevi St.
Tel. (03) 560 2223

With a cool name like Jewish Princess, you know it's got to be a good place. This funky neighborhood bar is a pleasant, quiet hangout.

Food

Jos & Los

51 Yehuda Halevi St.
Tel. (03) 560 6385

This funky restaurant with its flea market décor, indifferent service and limited copies of a daily menu typed by hand on thick, white paper is considered one of the coolest places in the city. The proprietor / chefs are famously lesbian and leftist, and the regular patrons include many of the city's Who's Who. Do arrive early, because they don't accept reservations and the items on the menu tend to disappear rapidly.

Books

Khotam Books

55 Sheinkin St.
Tel. (03) 685 2350

Most of the titles are in Hebrew, but there is a well-chosen selection of titles in English at this small, veteran bookshop. The soft-spoken proprietor is extremely knowledgeable and very helpful.

Design

Kisim

8 Hachashmal St.
Tel. (03) 560 4890

The unique, high-quality bags and wallets are characterized by clean, elegant lines and an attention to detail. Designer Yael Rosen-Ben Shachar opened her own boutique after establishing her reputation as a designer for chic shops in Israel and abroad.

Food

Kyoto

31 Montefiore St.
Tel. (03) 566 1234

Kyoto is a stylish, chic restaurant with a menu that combines traditional Japanese cuisine with elements from the South American kitchen to create colorful, unique and delicious fusion food.

Night & Shows

Levontin 7

7 Levontin St.
Tel. (03) 560 5084
www.myspace.com/levontine7

Musicians / proprietors Daniel Sarid and Assif Tsahar have created the most important, widely acclaimed music venue in Israel. Levontin 7 is a bar, café and performance space that hosts cutting edge live music acts from Israel and from all over the world – often just before they become truly famous in their own countries. Do check their website for upcoming performances.

Café

Loveat

1 Barzilay St.
Tel. (03) 566 6699

Famous for its home-roasted coffee beans, this stylish café is the place to stop for a break while shopping in Gan Hachashmal.

Café, Bakery

Mazzarin

42 Montefiore St.
Tel. (03) 566 7020

French-Austrian pastries are served in this chic and elegant patisserie / café. The building is gorgeous, and so is the décor.

Food

Mezze

51a Ahad Ha'am St.
Tel. (03) 629 9753

Simple, vegetarian, Levantine-influenced cuisine is served at this popular restaurant-café.

Food

Pasta Mia

10 Wilson St.
Tel. (03) 561 0189

Fresh, homemade pasta dishes are served in this cozy, intimate Italian restaurant.

Food

Pastis

73 Rothschild Blvd.
Tel. (03) 525 0773

Pastis has been serving Provençal-influenced cuisine to appreciative diners and food critics for more than a decade.

Food

Radio Rosco

97 Allenby St.
Tel. (03) 560 0334

Located in a charming inner courtyard that makes the noise of Allenby Street seem very far away, Radio Rosco serves delicious Italian dishes in a charming, fashionable setting.

Design

Rugine

46 Montefiore St.

Furniture and home accessories by the most exclusive and expensive international designers fill this multi-story building that was once a private residence.

Fashion

Shine

12 Harakevet St.
Tel. (03) 560 1658

Using pure, natural fabrics, the designer creates collections characterized by clean lines and neutral colors that are uniquely suited to the Tel Aviv climate and lifestyle.

Food

Stefan Braun

99 Allenby St.
Tel. (03) 560 4725

Located in a lovely old courtyard set back from noisy Allenby Street, Stefan Braun serves beautifully prepared Middle Eastern appetizers and meat dishes in a renovated Ottoman era building.

Café

Tachtit

9 Lincoln St.
Tel. (03) 561 8759

Tachtit means "underground" in Hebrew, which explains the symbols and maps of the London subway system that decorate this chic, 24-hour café. That, however, is where the connection with London ends. The kitchen serves upscale Tel Aviv café food, and the regular clientele ranges from scruffy Indy musicians and impecunious actors to famous television personalities and high tech businesspeople.

Design

Tes

12 Harakevet St.
Tel. (03) 560 1482

The beautifully designed bags at this chic little shop are sold all over the world. They tend to be oversized and constructed of high quality, unusual leathers.

Food

Vince & Tamar

10 Hatzfira St.
Tel. (03) 639 0407

Named for the husband and wife team who own it, this charming, idiosyncratic Italian restaurant is located in a rather grubby industrial area. The Swiss-born chef and his Israeli wife create gloriously unhealthy and delicious classic French dishes like sweetmeats, three-meat ragout with pasta and veal tongue.

Kitchen accessories

4 Chef

11 Carlebach St.
Tel. (03) 561 1803

This is where professional and amateur chefs come to purchase all the most exclusive kitchen accessories, from imported Italian espresso makers to Japanese knives. The knowledgeable staff is always happy to help you make your selection.

South End

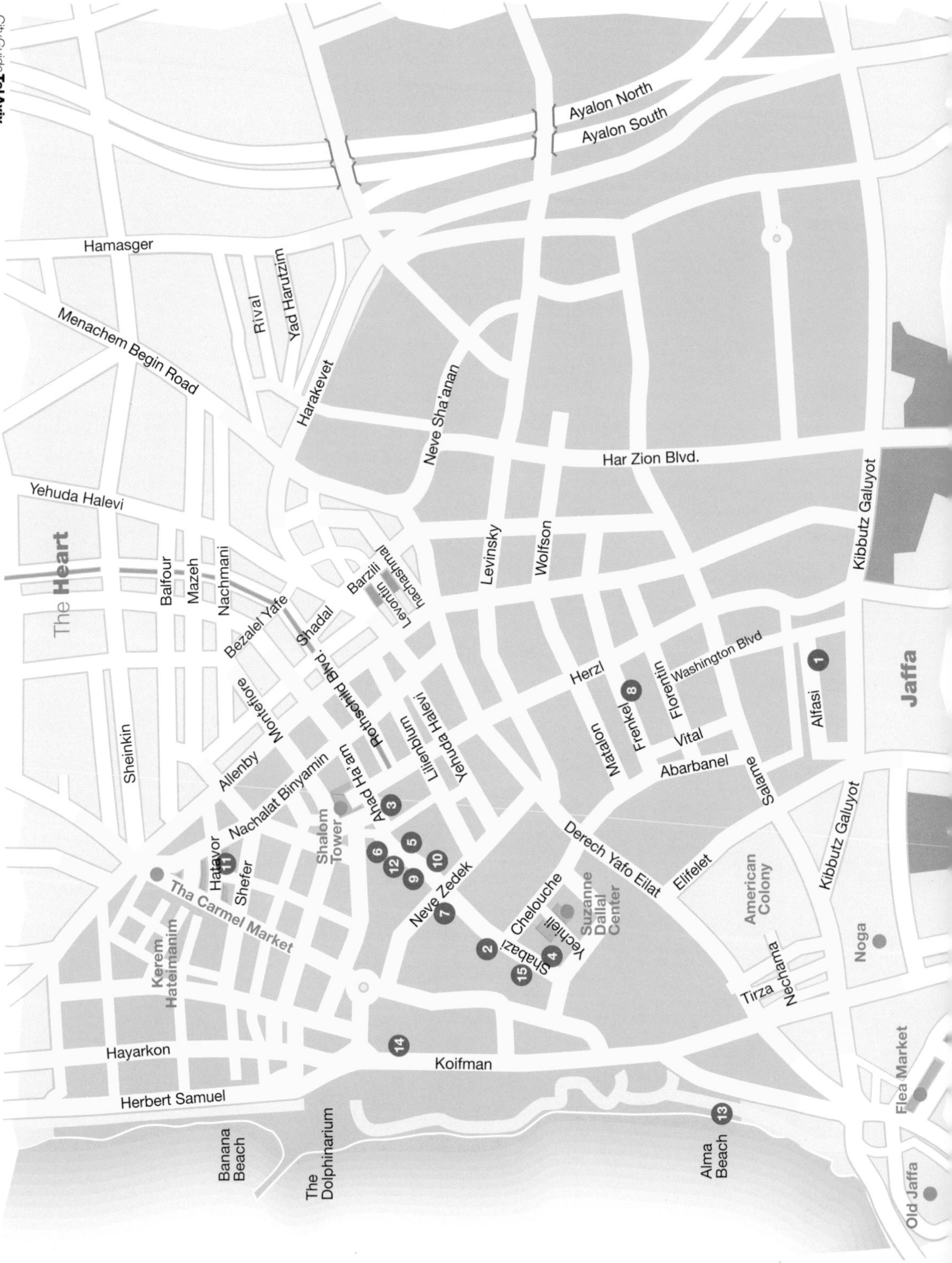

Ayalon North
Ayalon South
Hamasger
Rival
Yad Harutzim
Menachem Begin Road
Harakevet
Neve Sha'anan
Har Zion Blvd.
Yehuda Halevi
The Heart
Balfour
Mazeh
Nachmani
Bezalel Yafe
Shadal
Barzili
Levontin
Hachashmal
Levinsky
Wolfson
Kibbutz Galuyot
Rothschild Blvd.
Lilienblum
Yehuda Halevi
Montefiore
Sheinkin
Allenby
Nachalat Binyamin
Ahad Ha'am
Shalom Tower
Herzl
Frenkel
Florentin
Washington Blvd
Alfasi
Jaffa
Matalon
Vital
Abarbanel
Salame
Kibbutz Galuyot
Hatavor
Shefer
Tha Carmel Market
Neve Zedek
Derech Yafo Eilat
Elifelet
Chelouche
Yechieli
Shabazi
Suzanne Dallal Center
American Colony
Noga
Kerem Hateimanim
Tirza
Nechama
Hayarkon
Koifman
Herbert Samuel
Banana Beach
The Dolphinarium
Alma Beach
Flea Market
Old Jaffa
1
2
3
4
5
6
7
8
9
10
11
12
13
14
15

outh End

The neighborhoods that comprise the south end of Tel Aviv are amongst the city's oldest. Some, in fact, were established more than two decades before the founding of Tel Aviv – and then swallowed up during the 1930s and 1940s by the rapidly expanding city. Today the south end is partly gentrified, but mostly not.

It is full of all sorts of different markets, no-frills eateries serving traditional Turkish, Yemenite and Persian food, gloriously diverse architecture and some landmarks that date back to the city's very first decade. It also includes some of the city's best restaurants and most expensive real estate. The overall feeling in the south end is one of ethnic diversity, authenticity, history, urban grit and Levantine charm.

The residents of the south end are a mixed bunch. They range from urban hipsters and impecunious artists, to octogenarian Arabic-speaking Yemenite Jews and high-tech millionaires who have found refuge from the suburbs in Neve Tzedek – which has become one of Tel Aviv's most picturesque and sought after neighborhoods.

llenby St.

Given its very run-down look, it is difficult to believe that Allenby, which connects the south end to the heart of the city, was once Tel Aviv's most elegant street – its "grand boulevard." That was in the days of the British Mandate, from the 1920s to the late 1940s. Back then the section of Allenby that connected Rothschild to King George Street was the city's hub, its commercial center, known for its furriers, bookbinders, cafés and boutiques.

Today Allenby is noisy, dirty and seedy-looking. But look carefully behind the treetops and you will see some beautiful, though sadly neglected, old buildings from the 1920s. Some have a sign in mosaic tiles with the date on which it was built and the names of the architect and owner. Tel Aviv's Great Synagogue is located on Allenby, too. Lately, there are signs that Allenby may be on the cusp of a renaissance. There are a couple of good restaurants tucked away behind discreet signs and set back from the street; there are also a few interesting bars and some very good second-hand bookshops. Halper's, at 87 Allenby, has the widest selection of titles in English.

Herzl St.

Not far from Tel Aviv's first intersection, at Herzl and Rothschild, is an elaborate, rundown edifice known simply by its address - 16 Herzl Street. This was the city's first department store.

Just inside the entrance, the wall is adorned with the Hebrew word for "elevator," with a long, pointing finger painted above the word. The finger points at an old cast iron elevator – the city's first, although it no longer functions. One assumes there are plans to restore this striking building, which has featured in at least one well-known Israeli film – "Afula Express."

The white skyscraper that dominates Herzl Street on the other side of Rothschild Boulevard is the Shalom Tower, which was built on the site of the original Gymnasium Herzliya– the first high school with a curriculum taught entirely in Hebrew. Constructed in the 1970s, the Shalom Tower was once the tallest building in Israel, boasting a wax museum and an observation tower. Today its most interesting feature is located on the ground floor, where there is an elaborately detailed relief map of the city, with miniature buildings and other fascinating details that will keep adults and children equally engaged.

Neve Tzedek

Neve Tzedek (Oasis of Justice) is the city's oldest neighborhood. It is also its most beautiful, with an atmosphere that evokes an artists' colony or a small village.

Neve Tzedek was founded in 1887, 22 years before Tel Aviv, on land purchased by Aharon Chelouche. The Chelouche family, which emigrated from Algeria at the beginning of the nineteenth century, was one of the wealthiest and most prominent Jewish families in Jaffa; they were famous for their philanthropy and involvement in the Jewish community. Located on the street named after them, the Chelouche (pronounced and misspelled as "Shlush") family home in Neve Tzedek is now a museum.

During the first two decades of the twentieth century, Neve Tzedek was home to several prominent writers and authors. They included S.Y. Agnon, Israel's Nobel Laureate in literature, and the artist Nachum Gutman. Today Gutman's home, at 21 Rokach Street, is an excellent museum, with both permanent and changing exhibitions. There are also interactive exhibitions for children.

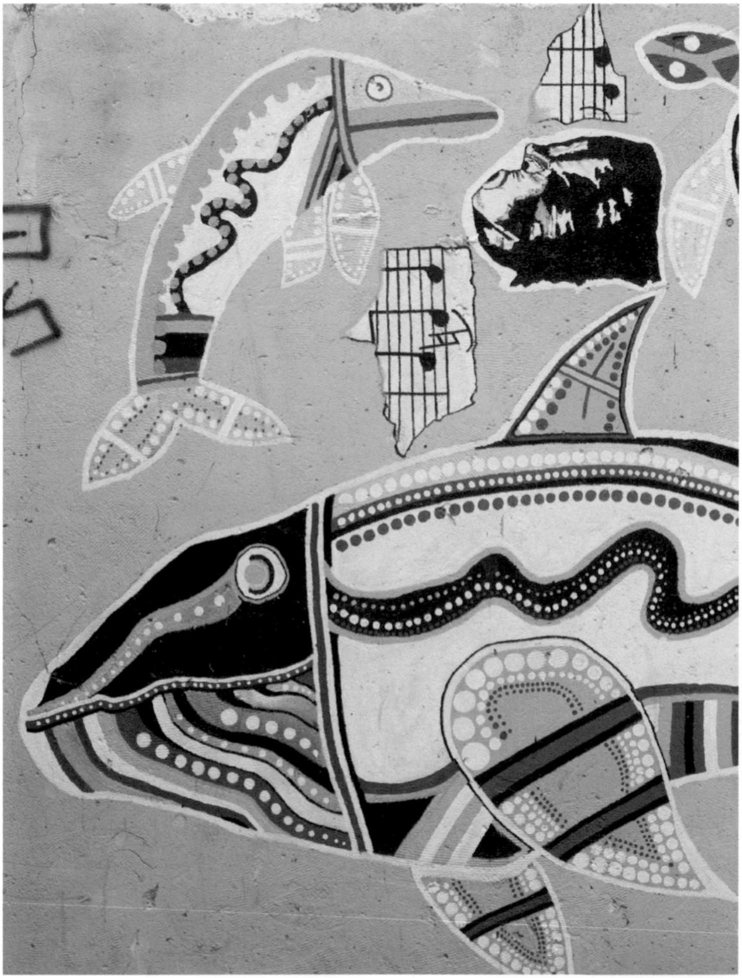

Shabazi Street, Neve Tzedek's longest thoroughfare, is lined with stylish cafés, restaurants, wine bars, boutiques and a variety of shops selling innumerable beautiful things. It is a lovely place to stroll, browse, shop or linger over a coffee. The beautiful, architecturally distinguished Suzanne Dellal Center is home to the world-renowned Batsheva Modern Dance Troupe. Its picturesque courtyards are a popular gathering place.

Following a prolonged period of decline, Neve Tzedek has, over the past two decades, been thoroughly gentrified. But it still has charm, authenticity and a relaxed neighborhood atmosphere. There are many old, unrenovated homes that are still inhabited by Yemenite families who moved into the area in the 1950s and refuse to sell their homes, to the chagrin of the real estate developers, because they are attached to their community, their lifestyle and their local synagogue.

Stroll around Neve Tzedek early on a quiet Saturday morning, and you're sure to hear traditional chanting emerging from the open windows of the old synagogues – like the tiny prayer house on Chelouche Street at the corner of Amzaleg Street, which has been in continuous use since the end of the nineteenth century.

The **Dolphinarium** and **Banana** Beach

The strip of beach that borders Neve Tzedek is called Banana Beach. Despite the pervasive smell of urine and rotting garbage in the parking lot of the area known as the Dolphinarium, which is now home to a fashionable outdoor bar in the summer months, Banana Beach is a popular hangout. It is also known as Drummer's Beach, for the amateur drummers who gather there on Friday afternoons at sunset for a "welcome to the weekend" jam session. Anyone can participate in the drumming, which continues until late at night and attracts jugglers, dancers and capoeira enthusiasts – as well as dozens of people who just come to enjoy the quintessentially laid back Tel Aviv atmosphere.

Directly across the street is Hassan Bek, the only functioning mosque on the Tel Aviv side of Tel Aviv-Jaffa. The muezzin juts up against the background of modern high-rise hotels, providing an oft-photographed contrast between old and new.

Just to the south, Charles Clore Park is a popular place to picnic – especially on Saturday afternoons, when dozens of families grill meat on portable barbecues and spit piles of empty sunflower seeds onto the grass while their children climb on the huge blue plastic jungle gym.

Alma Beach

Alma Beach, where the Manta Ray restaurant is located, has a little kiosk with a few outdoor seats. This is a particularly lovely place to stop in the late afternoon, order a coffee or a beer, and watch as the setting sun throws the ancient city of Jaffa into golden silhouette.

Lilienblum St.

Technically part of Neve Tzedek, Lilienblum is a side street that connects Allenby Street to Neve Tzedek's Pines (unfortunately pronounced "penis") Street. For years, until the 1970s, it was Israel's Wall Street. The Bank of Israel was headquartered on Lilienblum, as were the moneychangers who circumvented the country's then strict foreign currency trading laws.

The stock exchange moved up to Ahad Ha'am in the early 1970s; and later in the decade foreign currency regulations were lifted. As a result, Lilienblum lost its luster and became shabby and dull, with nothing to distinguish it but a few neglected buildings and dusty shops. But over the past decade it was rediscovered and renovated, and has rapidly become one of the main hubs of Tel Aviv's nightlife. Today Lilienblum is lined with hip lounge bars and fashionable restaurants, making it one of the best places to experience Tel Aviv's nightlife.

The **Nachalat Binyamin** Pedestrian Mall

Nachalat Binyamin is actually a very long street that extends deep into the Florentin neighborhood, but the section that parallels the Carmel Market, starting at Gruzenberg Street and curving up toward Allenby, opposite Sheinkin Street, is closed to vehicular traffic.

There are a few stylish bars and restaurants here, but the main reason to visit Nachalat Binyamin is the outdoor craft market on Tuesdays and Fridays, when it resembles market day in a medieval European city – with a Middle Eastern twist. On these days there are endless tables displaying an amazing variety of

HAWAIIAN

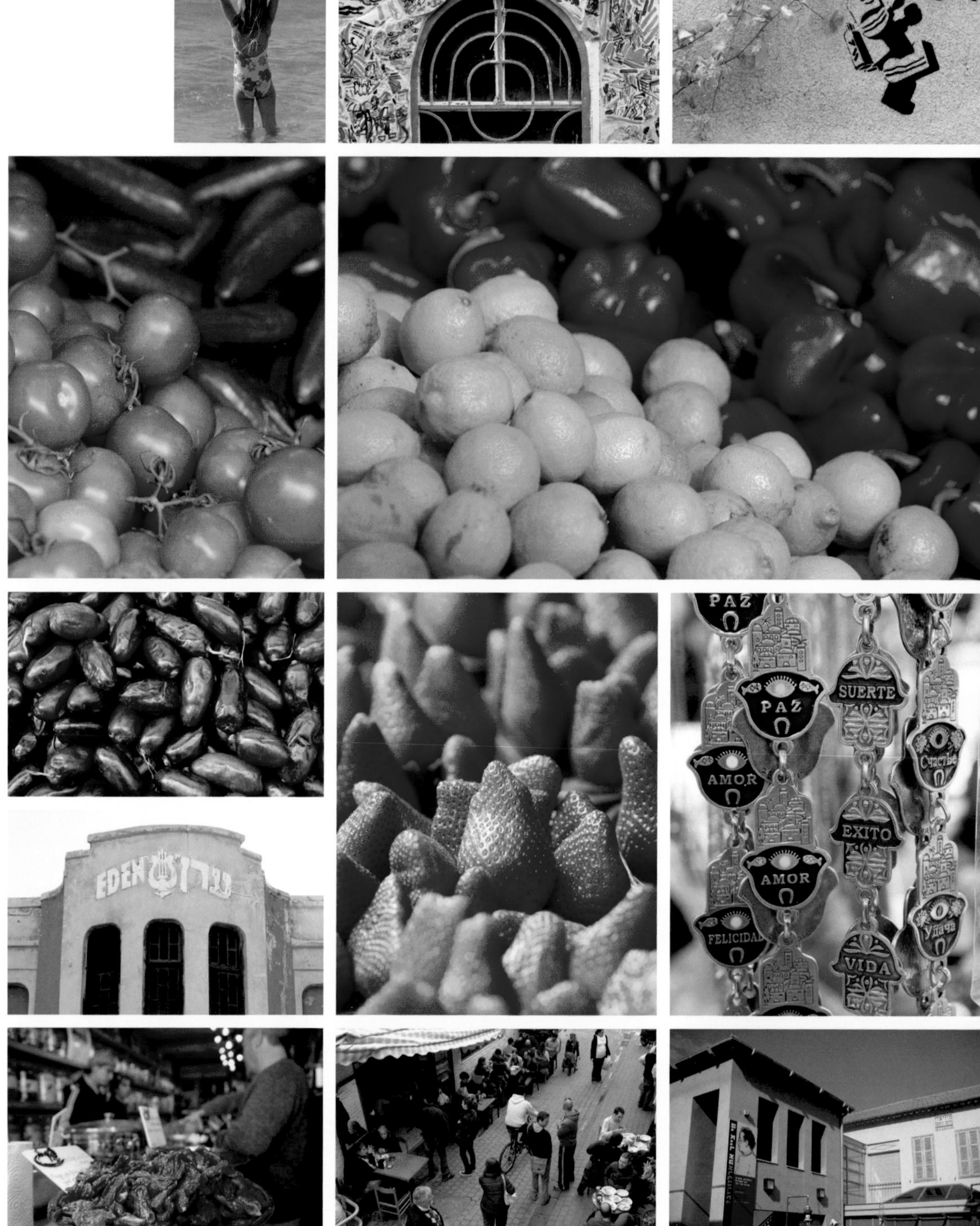
EDEN
PAZ
PAZ
SUERTE
AMOR
EXITO
AMOR
FELICIDAD
VIDA

arts and crafts. On Friday amateur musicians, acrobats and jugglers perform for delighted children. Do stop by the popular food stall staffed by a Druze family that sells enormous homemade flatbreads baked on the spot by a traditional method. Just follow your nose – you can't miss it.

The **Carmel** Market

The Carmel Market is the largest outdoor market in Tel Aviv. Its narrow, twisting streets are lined with stalls and shops selling everything from toiletries and clothes to meat and produce, all at rock-bottom prices. There are several Russian delicatessens that specialize in pork charcuterie, but the overwhelming majority of the shops and stands are owned by Israelis of North African descent, giving the market a distinctly "Mizrachi" (Eastern) flavor.

The shoppers, however, come from all over the world. This is the place to experience Israel's modern melting pot. The people who shop at the market include native-born Israelis, new immigrants and foreign workers from all over the globe – from China to Ghana. Many of the shops carry goods that cater to foreign workers, like fufu flakes, soya sauce and tofu. The best time to visit is midday on Friday, when the merchants of perishable goods lower their prices with loud shouts and the foreign workers, just released from work, come to buy food for the coming weekend.

Kerem Hateymanim
The Yemenite Vineyard

Founded in the 1930s by immigrants from Yemen (hence its name), the Kerem fell into decline in the decades following the establishment of the state, becoming known as an impoverished inner city ghetto. During the 1990s the municipality made some serious investments in the infrastructure; since then the winding streets have gradually been "discovered" by bohemian Tel Avivians looking for inexpensive housing, and many of the old buildings have been nicely renovated. Despite the influx of the artsy crowd, the area is still heavily populated by old-timers and hasn't lost its authenticity. If you're in the mood for some spicy Yemenite food in a no-frills environment, there are plenty of little restaurants to try. For hummus and other popular Middle Eastern dishes, Erez and Dror at 25 Malan Street is one of the most popular places to eat in the Kerem. It's a tiny place on a narrow street, just below the Carmel Market.

Florentin

Founded in 1927 by a Sephardic Jewish family from Salonika, Florentin began its existence as a middle class neighborhood for artisans and shopkeepers who had immigrated from Greece and Bulgaria. Due to rapid migration to the suburbs, Florentin was a neglected, borderline slum by the 1960s.

The decline of Florentin seemed to be on the cusp of a reverse in the early 1990s, when Eytan Fox, who went on to direct internationally acclaimed movies like “Yossi and Jagger,” “Walk on Water” and “The Bubble,” created a hit television series named for the neighborhood. The success of the series, which featured a group of twentysomething polyamorous artists and musicians living a cool, urban existence in a Levantine version of New York’s East Village, led many to predict Florentin’s imminent gentrification.

Fifteen years later, Florentin is teetering on the edge of major change – but its future is still uncertain. The residents are an interesting combination of hipster cool and solid, ethnic working class. Elegant, high-end furniture and home accessory shops have opened their doors over the last decade, particularly along Frenkel and Wolfson Streets, making Florentin a prime destination for top-end interior designers. Meanwhile, new luxury buildings are springing up all over the neighborhood. But there has been no significant investment in basic infrastructure like parking, road improvement and public transportation.

Florentin is definitely the place to experience Tel Aviv’s underground urban hipster nightlife scene. The apex of the scene is at Vital and Florentin Streets, where there is a jazz bar, a whiskey bar, a popular café and several trendy restaurants.

But the really edgy action is on the margins of Florentin. Check out the gay bar called ShaMa at 68 Herzl, on the corner of Wolfson Street, for example. Or there’s a low-key, cozy and cool bar that goes by the name Hudna (“truce” in Arabic) at 13 Abarbanel Street. Shiraleh, at 18 Yedidyah Frenkel Street, is a charming little cafe that doubles as an art gallery.

Other parts of Florentin remain traditional. The colorful food market on Levinsky Street is bursting with authenticity. Here you can find everything from exotic spices and dried fruit to freshly baked Turkish flatbread and cheese-filled

savory pastries. Most of the merchants are Jews from the Mediterranean basin; they still speak to one another in Ladino, or Judaeo-Spanish.

There are several excellent, traditional Persian and Turkish restaurants on the stretch of Nachalat Binyamin, between Jaffa Road and Levinsky Street, which are definitely worth a visit – especially if you are looking for local color. Sharing tables during peak hours is the norm at these casual, Levantine eateries.

Many of Florentin's streets are devoted to a single product – such as bedroom furniture, kitchen accessories, cheap clothing and lighting fixtures. There are also streets devoted to a single craft, like carpentry or upholstering. The local merchants have known each other for decades, with many passing on the business from one generation to the next. As a result, there is a unique culture based on shared experience, history – and even, in some cases, terminology.

Sadly, the traditional Florentin culture is on the cusp of dying out. The family businesses are in the third generation; many offspring have decided to branch out into their own professions; meanwhile, the municipality is trying to push out the wholesale merchants because of overcrowding. So far the merchants have successfully opposed this move, but in the end the municipality will probably win. Now is really the time to visit Florentin in order to witness and experience the last years of a thriving, colorful and traditional lifestyle.

Neve Shaanan

Neve Shaanan will fascinate amateur urban anthropologists – as long as they are not afraid of a little grit and chaos. This clamorous, neglected neighborhood is home to Tel Aviv's urban underclass. It is where foreign workers from Ghana, Liberia, China, Romania the Philippines and Thailand live side-by-side with prostitutes, drug dealers and narcotics addicts.

The area known as the Old Central Bus Station is packed with shops that cater to the foreign workers, while the nearby pedestrian mall is where they come to relax and have a beer at one of the cheap outdoor pubs on Friday afternoons, when the weekend begins.

[Map 1]

Design

Kastiel & Sons Design Center

36 Alfasi St.
Tel. (03) 683 6334

Kastiel is one of the most exclusive international names in custom design furniture and interior design. The original six-level Florentin showroom was established 66 years ago by Efraim Kastiel. The family maintained the business in the Florentin location until 2008, when they moved to an enormous new space on Alfasi Street in southern Tel Aviv.
Designed by Alex Meitlis, the new site is an old textile factory that has been transformed into a striking single floor showroom that spreads out over 3,400 meters, and is surrounded by a courtyard.
Kastiel is the place to buy beautiful custom designed furniture for your home in Israel or abroad. The showroom is packed with garden furniture and Viking professional domestic appliances. The unique accessories, paintings and rugs are original works of art.
The internationally renowned Kastiel team provides complete interior design services.

Fashion

Mayu

15 Shabazi St.
Tel. (03) 516 6975
61 Ussishkin St., Ramat HaSharon
Tel. (03) 549 9033

[Map 2]

Located in a renovated nineteenth century residence, Mayu in Neve Tzedek is the newest branch of designer Maya Zukerman's boutiques.

Mayu's rapid proliferation is testimony to the designer's deep understanding of the city's Zeitgeist and fashion outlook. She expresses it perfectly with her collections of casual and style-conscious clothes and accessories that are sexy in an appealingly understated manner. The fabrics are all natural fibers – primarily cotton and wool. They breathe, making them well suited to the long, hot and humid summers. They also work beautifully as layers during the brief, but chilly and damp, rainy season. For the Neve Tzedek branch, Mayu showcases the most muted and delicate colors of her collections. Somehow, this seems appropriate for Neve Tzedek's contemporary-yet-traditional atmosphere. This branch of Mayu also showcases a selection of lovely jewelry, in addition to a wide selection of accessories.

Define simple

Design

Tali's Lifestyle Design, by Tali Sebbag

8 Ahad Ha'am St.
Tel. (03) 510 8848

[Map 3]

Designer Tali Sebbag's showroom is an intimate, luxurious space that is a hymn of praise to elegance and style, providing the atmosphere and inspiration for creating elegant home and workspace décor and lifestyle design. Having established a reputation as a boutique events designer for the fashionable elite, Tali opened her showroom in order to display the beautiful lifestyle accessories that she designs or selects during her frequent trips to Europe. The range of items includes exclusive French home and body scents, silver tea and coffee services, elegant dresses and separates, designer jewelry, lamps, cushions, and customized flower arrangements. In addition to her work in home and lifestyle design, Tali continues to design intimate boutique events for her loyal clientele.

Food

Dallal

10 Shabazi St.
Tel. (03) 510 9292
www.dallal.info

[Map 4]

Located in a beautifully renovated, late nineteenth-century home in Neve Tzedek, Dallal has been one of the most popular restaurants in Tel Aviv since its opening day. With its casual-yet-chic approach to eating out, Dallal expresses perfectly the tastes of stylish Tel Avivians. The unpretentious food is imaginatively prepared, the service is efficient, and the décor fuses the elegance and comfort of European mock-chic with Levantine warmth. These elements combine to create a relaxing and thoroughly enjoyable atmosphere.

Some of the most appealing aspects of Dallal are in the details. The custom-designed club-style chairs are wonderfully comfortable, and the leather banquettes are reminiscent of a Parisian brasserie. The wine list, which places an emphasis on Israeli boutique wines, offers a wide range of expensive vintages by the glass. The bread and French breakfast pastries are baked on the premises, and are available for takeaway at the Dallal bakery next door. The breakfast menu - eggs benedict, blintzes and the traditional Israeli breakfast – are served all day. Even the coffee elicits a sigh of pleasure – which is saying a lot in this coffee-mad city. Or, if you prefer tea to coffee, stop by during the late afternoon for a classic English high tea.

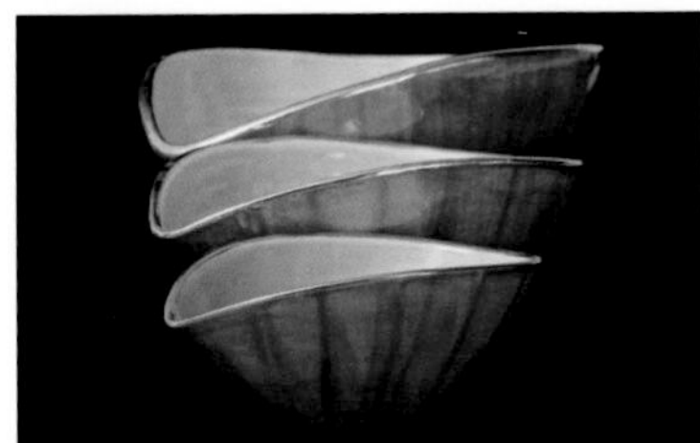

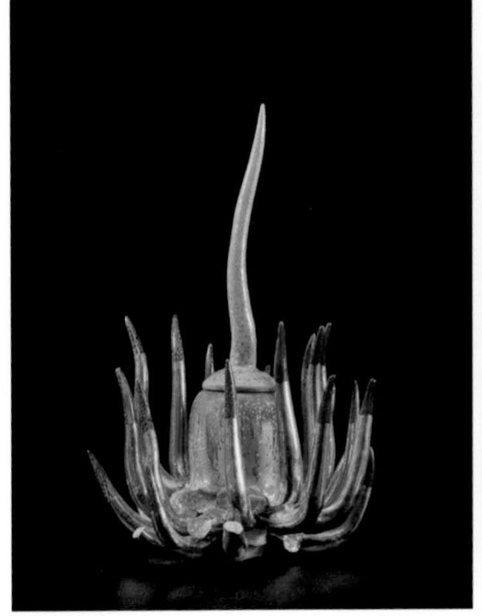

[Map 5]

Design

Samy D

56 Shabazi St.
Tel. (03) 516 4968
www.samy-d.com

French-born Israeli artist Samy D's stunningly beautiful ceramic dishes and objects have been featured in some of the world's most prestigious fashion and design magazines. With a technique he developed himself, Samy D combines deep, vibrant color, 14-karat gold and delicate designs in a manner that has revolutionized the world of ceramics. Art critics are hard-pressed to find sufficient superlatives to describe Samy D's creations, which are sought after by discerning collectors. His works are sold at the most exclusive shops in the world. They are also displayed at art galleries, solo exhibitions and museums both in Israel and abroad.
Samy D designs custom-made items for select private customers and prestigious corporations such as Microsoft Holland and Bank Hapoalim. For El Al Israel Airlines, Samy D was commissioned to design the breakfast service for First Class passengers.

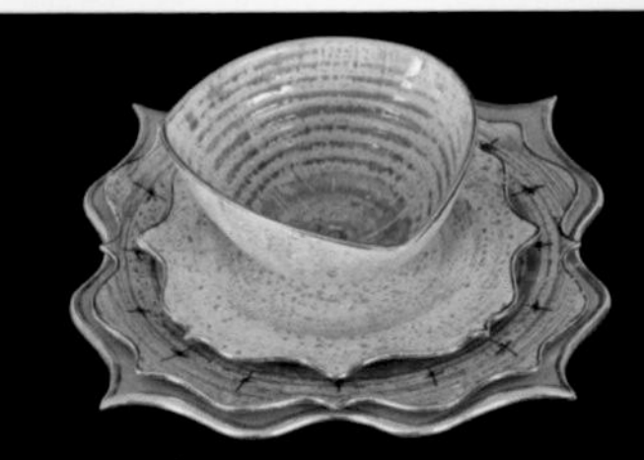

Cafe, Chocolatier

Café Mia & Dolce Mia

55 Shabazi St.
Tel. (03) 516 8793

[Map 6]

This wood-accented, cozy café on upper Shabazi Street, is one of the most charming in Neve Tzedek. Mia Café is popular with tourists, yet retains its neighborhood atmosphere and is a favorite hangout with the local artistic/bohemian community.
The menu features popular café food – quiches, salads, sandwiches and the famous Israeli breakfast – all prepared with a tasty fusion of Mediterranean and European culinary influences. The Israeli breakfast, for instance, is served with homemade, sesame-studded Turkish flatbread.
Dolce Mia has a gorgeous array of homemade chocolate confections, made with gourmet chocolate from Israeli boutique chocolateries.

Hotel, Café

Nina Café Suites Hotel

29 Shabazi St.
Tel. (03) 516 1767 - Café
(052) 508 4141 - Hotel reservations
www.ninacafehotel.com

Easily identified by its distinctive red-and-white striped awning, Nina is an homage to the old-fashioned French village café. Free WiFi and excellent espresso are standard in Tel Aviv; but Nina's sandwiches, served on homemade baguettes, are a cut above.
The Nina Café Suites Hotel is a home away from home for discerning travelers seeking luxury and intimacy. Each suite is decorated in exquisite taste, with furniture, artwork and Afghan silk rugs selected either from Neve Tzedek boutiques or from markets abroad. Thoughtful details include l'Occitane bath products, plush robes, slippers, a large bottle of Evian water, fresh seasonal fruit, fresh flowers, a selection of films on DVD, and daily newspapers in a variety of languages. The well-appointed kitchen is equipped with a full range of cooking implements. Additional amenities include free WiFi, flat screen television and DVD player. Breakfast is served all day, either in the café or in the guest's room. Bicycles are available for those who wish to explore the city using pedal power.
The Nina Boutique stocks a selection of stylish casual clothes and shoes for women, a range of luxury bath and body products, and an eclectic range of unique and quirky souvenirs.

[Map 7]

Design

BaBoo

34 Yedidia Frenkel St.
Tel. (03) 682 8885
www.be-baboo.com

[Map 8]

Located in the heart of Florentin's most fashionable area, BaBoo showcases an eclectic and innovative collection of handmade lamps and light fixtures. The shop's beautiful interior design is seductively cozy, yet pleasingly uncluttered. The low-key light projected through lampshades of various delicate colors creates an atmosphere of sensual warmth that draws passersby in, inviting them to linger, explore and ask questions.

BaBoo's unique style defies classification. Some of the lamps are indisputably modern, while others show Oriental and Baroque influences. One of their most striking modern lampshades is created out of film stock that is printed with evocative, colorful abstract designs.

Owners Eli Sagi and Billy Berger travel regularly to Venice, Paris, Milan and Istanbul in order to find unusual and high quality materials for their constantly evolving and changing collection. Lamps can be purchased off the shelves, or ordered custom-made.

Design

Agas and Tamar

43 Shabazi St.
Tel. (03) 516 8421
www.agasandtamar.com

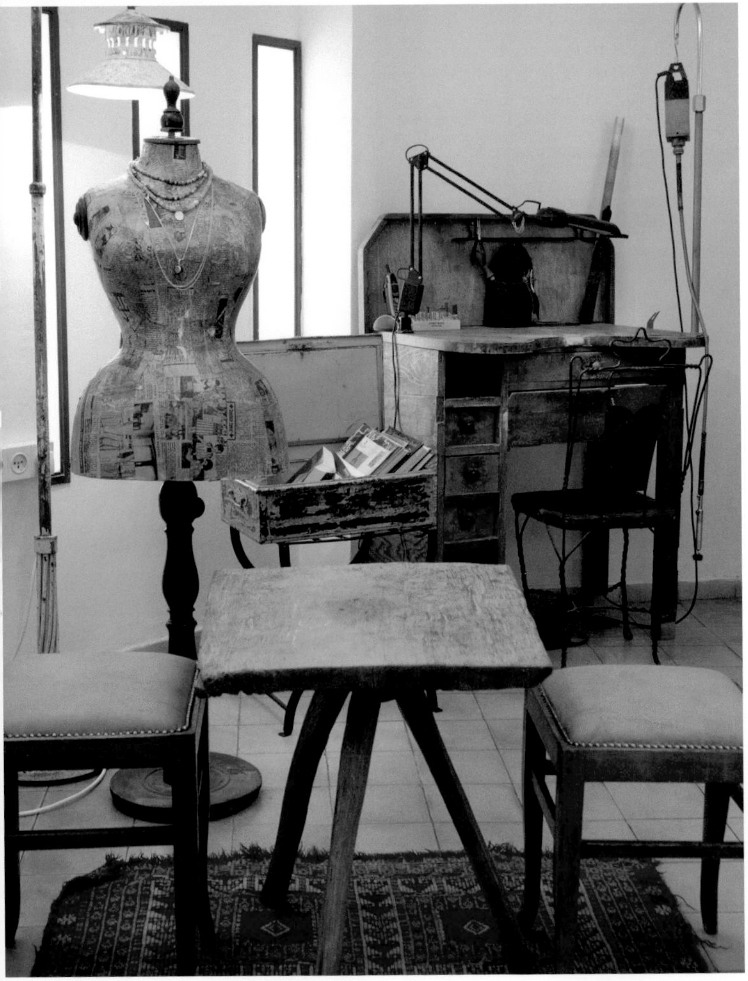

Agas and Tamar merges the names of designer/proprietors Einat Agassi and Tamar Harel-Klein. The words also mean "pear and date," which is not a coincidence. With the name of their charming studio boutique in Neve Tzedek, the artists are expressing their driving philosophy of synergizing natural materials with artisanship in jewelry design, and in merging inspiration from the past with a classic, modern sensibility.

Using matte gold, precious and semi-precious stones, Einat and Tamar create bracelets, necklaces, earrings, rings and cufflinks for both men and women. With their clean lines and understated luxury, Agas and Tamar creations have long been instantly recognizable amongst Tel Aviv jewelry lovers.

Recently, Agas and Tamar have gained recognition in prestigious international fashion publications. The opening of a branch in New York's fashionable SoHo area is testament to their rapidly growing international fame.

[Map 9]

Books

Sipur Pashut

36 Shabazi St.
Tel. (03) 510 7040
www.sipurpashut.net

Named after the Hebrew title of Nobel laureate S.Y. Agnon's novel A Simple Story, Sipur Pashut is one of the jewels of Neve Tzedek, which in 1925 was home to Agnon and other important intellectuals. Nestled between the galleries and cafés of Shabazi Street, this independent bookshop serves as a voice of Israeli literature with its monthly author readings, book launches and children's story hours. Its English language section features a wide range of individually selected fiction and non-fiction titles, including art and design books, children's books, feminist literature, magazines and periodicals. The helpful, well-read staff speak excellent English and serve international customers through their website.

[Map 10]

Food

[Map 11]

Carmella Bistro

46 Hatavor St.
Tel. (03) 516 1417

Housed in a stunningly romantic, restored early twentieth-century building near the Carmel Market, Carmella Bistro is one of the jewels of the Tel Aviv dining scene. Critics heap superlatives on Chef Daniel Zach's imaginative, lovingly presented Mediterranean cuisine.

Chef Zach chose the location of his restaurant for its proximity to the market, which he visits daily for inspiration and the freshest possible ingredients, from which he creates a very appealing tasting menu. Carmella offers the most comprehensive list of Israeli wines in the country, including boutique wineries and limited edition vintages.

Jewelry

Orit Ivshin

53 Shabazi St.
Tel. (03) 516 0811
www.oritivshin.co.il

Orit Ivshin creates jewelry that is well suited to the traditional-yet-contemporary character of Neve Tzedek, the neighborhood in which her charming studio shop is located. Working by hand, the artist creates modern jewelry with traditional influences, successfully merging past and present in an expression of timeless beauty. Neither bulky nor overly delicate, Orit Ivshin's creations appeal to a wide range of art and jewelry lovers who appreciate simplicity, individualism and high quality. Her pieces seem to take on the wearer's character, complementing it with a quiet statement of personal style.

[Map 12]

Food

Manta Ray

Alma Beach, near the Etzel Museum
Tel. (03) 517 4773
www.mantaray.co.il

Put together an attractive beachfront location, impeccably fresh seafood prepared with a distinctly Mediterranean flavor, casually friendly but efficient waiters and you have the winning combination that has made Manta Ray one of the most popular restaurants in Tel Aviv. The food is perfectly and frequently memorably prepared, and the murmuring of the waves provides a particularly pleasant backdrop to outdoor dining. An old-fashioned wood-burning iron stove provides cozy warmth during the chilly and damp winter.

A wide variety of mezze (Middle Eastern appetizers), called "mazzetim" in Hebrew, are attractively presented on massive round platters, allowing patrons to choose the ones that look most appealing. Homemade flatbread is served as an accompaniment. For those who prefer meat to fish and seafood, there are several excellent choices. Granola and fresh fruit supplement the traditional Israeli breakfast, served daily from 9 A.M. until noon.

[Map 13]

[Map 14]

Food

Herbert Samuel

6 Koifman St., Beit Gibor
Tel. (03) 516 6516
www.herbertsamuel.co.il

Jonathan Roshfeld has for years been one of Israel's best-known celebrity haute-cuisine chefs. No wonder, then, that Herbert Samuel has been a roaring success since its opening night. The exciting, Italian-influenced cuisine that comes out of the open kitchen upstairs has garnered rave reviews from both international and local food critics, with Herbert Samuel named Restaurant of the Year for 2007 by Time Out Tel Aviv, and by Israel's two mass circulation daily newspapers. There is rarely an empty chair around the enormous wooden bar, where diners can enjoy a variety of light meals composed of appetizers, and tables are booked well in advance. Expect to see a Who's Who of prominent local personalities scattered amongst the diners.

[Map 15]

Food, Café

Suzanna

9 Shabazi St.
Tel. (03) 517 7580

Suzanna has long been one of the most popular cafes in Neve Tzedek. An enormous ficus tree spreads its branches over the outdoor patio, shading diners as they enjoy Middle Eastern specialties like stuffed vegetables, kubbeh soup and perfectly grilled local fish. A cooling breeze blows during the long, hot summer afternoons, making this a particularly lovely place to linger over a coffee and a pre-dinner snack. During the summer drinks and finger food are served on the rooftop bar, with its views of Neve Tzedek and the Mediterranean. Come winter, the Ottoman-era interior becomes a cozy refuge in which to enjoy a hot apple cider or a satisfying bowl of Moroccan harira soup.

More of the Best

Night

Abraxas

40 Lilienblum St.
Tel. (03) 510 4435

More than a decade after it pioneered the dance bar scene on Lilienblum Street, Abraxas is still one of the most popular lounge and dance bars in the city. It hosts excellent DJs and recently placed its kitchen under the supervision of star chef Rafi Cohen.

Design

Arik Ben Simhon

110 Nachalat Binyamin St.
Tel. (03) 683 7865

Arik Ben Simhon is one of the biggest names in the Israeli design scene. The Ben Simhon look is unmistakably modern, but also timeless.

Night

Artemis

52 Nachalat Binyamin St.
Tel. (03) 510 0663

It's loud, it's crazy, it's sexy and it's an all-night scene with dancing on the bar and wild energy all around. This two-story bar is a hot and happening scene that grabs you by the throat the minute you walk in the door.

Jewelry

Ayala Bar

36 Shabazi St.
Tel. (03) 510 0082

Created from beads and silk threads, Ayala Bar's colorful and artistic costume jewelry is exotic and arresting.

Children's Fashion

Babette

31 Shabazi St.
Tel. (03) 510 0534

Situated in the charming Neve Tzedek quarter, this charming boutique specializes in the most exclusive European designers for children's clothes.

Food, Night

Bugsy

26 Florentin St.
Tel. (03) 681 3138

Café by day and bar scene by night, Bugsy is a Florentin institution that attracts a loyal crowd of regulars throughout the week and partiers on the weekend.

Food

Catit

4 Heichal Hatalmud St.
Tel. (03) 510 7001

In the space of one month, chef Meir Adoni won the local version of Iron Chef and was named the city's best chef by Time Out Tel Aviv, which also declared Catit the city's best restaurant. Located in a beautifully renovated Ottoman-era residence, this French-Mediterranean restaurant is currently considered one of the best in the country.

Food, Café

Casco – Urban Lab

3 Florentin St.
Tel. (03) 518 2144
www.cascotelaviv.com

Combining food and art, Casco is a restaurant that also hosts art exhibitions and performance art in this charming, intimate, candle-lit space.

Night

Clara

1 Koifman St., Dolphinarium area
Tel. (03) 510 2060

Located right on the water, Clara is the quintessential summer bar / hangout for rich kids with white teeth from the northern suburbs and tanned French ex-pats.

Hotel

David Intercontinental

12 Koifman St.
Tel. (03) 795 1111

Madonna stays here when she visits Tel Aviv for the annual Kabbalah Conference. The David Intercontinental Hotel is one of Tel Aviv's veteran five-star hotels, with the usual range of amenities one would expect at an expensive luxury hotel.

Pilates

Dror Raz Pilates

5 Yechieli St., Suzanne Dellal Center
Tel. (03) 510 8527
www.pilates.co.il

Located in the Suzanne Dellal compound, the Dror Raz Pilates center is a lovely place to get fit. It is also acclaimed as the best Pilates center in Israel.

Food

Floyd

10 Shefer St.
Tel. (077) 810 1033

Located at the edge of the bustling Carmel Market, Floyd is a fashionable and popular seafood and pasta bistro.

Design

Hadarim

48 Salame St.
Tel. (03) 681 0678

This multi-story design shop sells imaginative and attractive home accessories. Browsing is a very enjoyable experience.

Design

Hafatzim

27 Chelouche St.
Tel. (03) 517 8744

Charming home accessories and eclectic, tasteful furniture are sold at this attractive shop in the heart of Neve Tzedek.

Night

Ha'oman 17

88 Abarbanel St.
Tel. (03) 681 3636

Ha'Oman 17 became the hottest club in the country when it was located in Jerusalem. But for some reason the cachet didn't translate too well when it moved to Tel Aviv. It's still one of the biggest nightclubs in the city, and certainly worth a visit, but it's not the heart of the nightlife scene.

Yoga

Iyengar Yoga Center

2 Chelouche St.
Tel. (03) 516 3641

The instructors here were trained in Mysore at the yoga school headed by famed guru BKS Iyengar.

Night

Jajo

47 Shabazi St.
Tel. (03) 516 4557

There is rarely an empty seat at this popular wine bar.

Food

Kimmel

6 Hasha'ar St.
Tel. (03) 510 5204

Kimmel has been serving traditional Provençal cuisine for more than a decade. The critics still approve, and so do the loyal patrons.

Night

Lenny's

7 Vital St.
Tel. (03) 518 6637

Café by day and bar by night, Lenny's is always a pleasant place to hang out.

Night

Lima Lima

42 Lilienblum St.
Tel. (03) 560 0924

Nearly a decade after it became one of the first lounge bars on Lilienblum Street, Lima Lima still attracts a hip young crowd.

Night

Minerva

98 Allenby St.
Tel. (03) 560 5595

Tel Aviv is so ridiculously gay friendly that there's really no need for homosexuals to ghettoize themselves. But sometimes a gay girl just feels like hanging out with other gay girls. That's when she goes to Minerva.

Night

Mishmish

17 Lilienblum St.
Tel. (03) 516 8178

Old fashioned cocktails for a more grownup crowd are served in this gently lit, cozy and stylish bar.

Fashion

Mizo

51 Shabazi St.
Tel. (03) 516 4105

Inbal Ben Zakan is a former dancer turned fashion designer who creates unique, deeply stylish clothes that move with the body and bear more than a passing nod to the influence of Issey Miyake.

Food

Nana Bar

1 Ahad Ha'am St.
Tel. (03) 516 1915

With its romantic atmosphere and delicious food, Nana Bar has been a favorite for more than a decade.

Food, Night

Nanuchka

28 Lilienblum St.
Tel. (03) 516 2254

The Georgian food served at this gloriously eccentric restaurant is absolutely delicious and not to be missed. At night the bar area becomes the main draw, with excellent DJs on some nights, and live performances of eclectic music styles ranging from oud to klezmer on other nights. Dancing on the bar is common.

ood

NG

Ahad Ha'am St.
el. (03) 516 7888

:arnivores of the world unite at NG, where ome of the city's best steaks are served to n appreciative crowd.

:e cream

Savta Ice Cream

Yechieli St.
el. (03) 510 5545

avta means "grandmother" in Hebrew - vhich is appropriate, given that this veteran omemade ice cream outlet has been round for decades.

Vhisky bar

Satchmo

Vital St.

erious whisky lovers come here to imbibe heir favorite blends and single malts.

Design

Serendipity Lifestyle gallery

30 Chelouche St.
el. (03) 516 6045

The lucky tendency to find interesting or aluable things by chance

Night

Shesek

17 Lilienblum St.
Tel. (03) 516 9520

Shesek has been around for a long time by Tel Aviv standards, but it is still one of the hippest lounge bars in the city. The vibe here is particularly good toward mid-week, after midnight, when some of the country's best DJs spin excellent funk and groove.

Food

Tahel

30 Nachalat Binyamin St.
Tel. (03) 516 8410

The atmosphere is intimate and relaxing at this charming Spanish tapas and wine bar.

Ice cream

Tartufo

25 Shabazi St.
Tel. (03) 517 0505

Bringing the craze of Sicilian ice cream to Neve Tzedek, Tartufo serves a wide range of delicious homemade flavors to appreciative locals.

Café

Taza D'Oro

6 Ahad Ha'am St.
Tel. (03) 516 6329

Once the best café in Neve Tzedek, Taza d'Oro has far too much competition these days. But the coffee is still good, and the courtyard is a charming place to sit and enjoy live jazz performances on Friday afternoons.

Jaffa

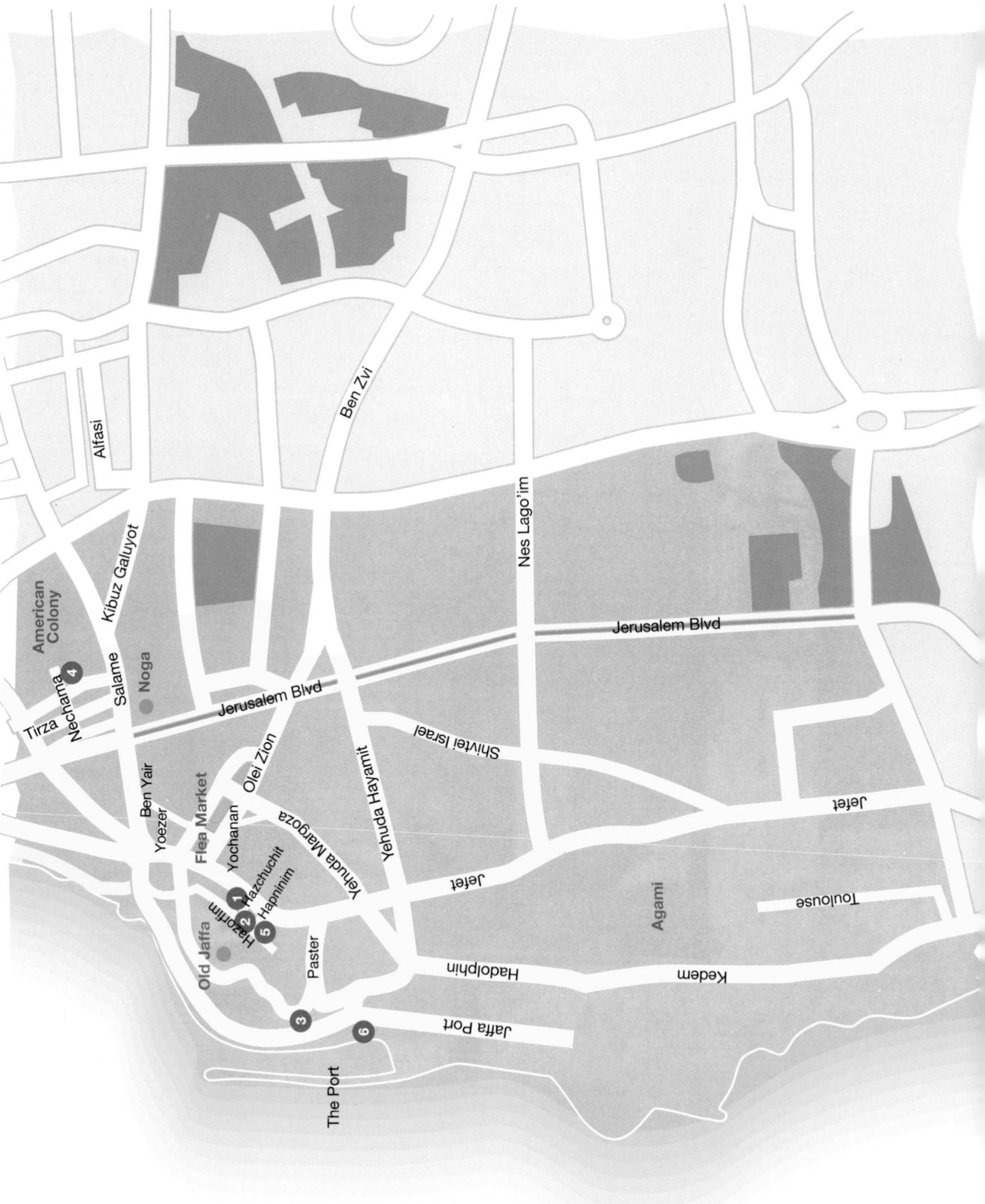

American Colony
Tirza
Nechama
4
Salame
Kibuz Galuyot
Alfasi
Ben Yair
Yoezer
Noga
Old Jaffa
Flea Market
Hazorfim
1
2
5
Yochanan
Hazchuchit
Hapninim
Olei Zion
Jerusalem Blvd
3
Paster
Yehuda Margoza
The Port
6
Yehuda Hayamit
Ben Zvi
Jaffa Port
Hadolphin
Jefet
Shivtei Israel
Nes Lago'im
Agami
Kedem
Toulouse
Jefet
Jerusalem Blvd

Jaffa

Jaffa (Yafo in Hebrew, Yaffa in Arabic) is historically, culturally and anthropologically rich, offering so many things to do and see that one could easily devote a couple of days to exploring its many landmarks, hidden side streets, historical sites, different neighborhoods, restaurants and shops.

This ancient city can effectively be divided into two sections : the old city, which has been restored and turned into a popular tourist attraction; and the newer part of the city, which has a population that is ethnically and economically diverse.

Old Jaffa has a picturesque ancient port, historic sites, restored houses dating back to the Ottoman period and clusters of upscale restaurants, galleries and shops. It is a major tourist attraction for both foreigners and Israelis, with the latter descending upon the city in droves to eat hummus, shop at the flea market and stroll the alleys on Fridays, Saturdays and Jewish holidays.

The newer part of Jaffa is mostly residential. Its residents are a heterogeneous mix of Muslims, Christians and Jews, with the latter divided between financially comfortable young people and relatively impoverished old-timers who have been living in the area since the 1950's. Much of residential Jaffa shows the municipality's neglect and the residents' poverty, but there are several areas that have been beautifully maintained by old middle class families who have lived there for generations, or gentrified by an influx of artists and professionals. Ajami in particular boasts many beautiful old homes and impressive landmarks, green parks, lovely views, some good local restaurants and an authentic neighborhood atmosphere.

History

Jaffa is often referred to as the oldest functioning port in the world. But while it was a busy commercial port from the Bronze Age until the early 1930's, today it is a sleepy, run-down but picturesque marina used by local fisherman and yachtsmen.

The ancient city above the port has a rich and violent history of conquest and re-conquest, destruction and reconstruction. It is mentioned in both the Hebrew and Christian Bibles, and was used by King Solomon to import cedars from Tyre for the building of the First Temple. Subsequent rulers include the

Arabs, starting from 636 C.E., the Crusaders five centuries later, the Ottomans, the Egyptian Mamluks and then the Ottomans again. When Napoleon conquered the city in 1799, he infamously drowned 2,000 Albanian prisoners in the harbor. All these historical events are noted and summarized on plaques at various sites in the refurbished port area.

From the mid-19th century until the British conquest in 1917, the city was a thriving commercial hub of the Ottoman Empire. Its diverse population of Muslims, Christians and Jews, who engaged in commerce, banking, fishing and manufacturing, swelled to the point of overcrowding by the beginning of the early twentieth century. From the late nineteenth century until the 1920s, Jaffa was the headquarters of the modern Zionist movement in Israel. During the Arab Uprising of 1936-1939 there were several violent riots in Jaffa. As a result, most of the British and Jewish businesses moved to Tel Aviv.

While neighboring Tel Aviv was originally established in 1909 as a suburb of Jaffa, it grew rapidly and eventually dwarfed the ancient city. In 1950, it was incorporated into Tel Aviv, creating the municipality of Tel Aviv-Jaffa.

And yet, while the two cities are nominally one, they look and feel utterly different. This is partly, of course, because Jaffa is old and Tel Aviv is new. But it is also because Jaffa still has a heterogeneous population of Arabs and Jews living side-by-side. Tel Aviv has a large minority of non-Jewish residents, but few Arabs live there.

The **port city**

The ancient port city is clearly visible from Tel Aviv. Built on a hill overlooking the water, it juts out from the coastline and looks, from a distance, like a fortress – which it was, once. It also offers a spectacular view of Tel Aviv. Today the port is undergoing an extensive renovation process that will make it into an attractive gathering place for locals and tourists alike.

One of the most picturesque ways to approach Jaffa is by foot, along the beachfront promenade, across the pedestrian bridge that unofficially marks the place where it meets Tel Aviv – where the old city meets the new. This route will take you directly into the refurbished port area, with its lovely views and

תל אביב-יפו

many historical sites that are clearly marked with signs and arrows.

Notable sites include the Rock of Andromeda, the Zodiac Alleys, the Clock, the Mahmoudia Mosque, Street Peter's Church, Kedumim Square, the Libyan Synagogue (now a museum) and the archaeological excavations at Jaffa Hill. Since they are all clustered close together, it is easy to see them in a leisurely half day of exploring.

There are many galleries, restaurants, museums and shops in old Jaffa. The area is small and well marked, so there is really no need to list them here – although the Ilana Goor Museum is particularly recommended. Otherwise, you will inevitably discover most landmarks just by walking around the area. The restaurants facing the water are a bit pricey and sometimes a tad touristy, but not overly so. And given the view and the setting, it's easy to overlook these minor drawbacks.

Not all the restaurants overlook the water, however. Opposite the Clock Tower there are several excellent restaurants, cafes and bars tucked away in the stone alleys and on the side streets of the Noga Quarter. If you are more interested in good food than the view, these places might be a better choice – especially for dinner.

During the summer months, the Tel Aviv municipality often sponsors live musical performances in the square outside St. Peter's Church. There are schedules posted and distributed around the square, or on the municipality website.

The streets, named after the signs of the Zodiac, are lined with galleries and artists' studios, as well as shops selling jewelry, Judaica and souvenirs that are, surprisingly, not too tacky.

The **flea market**

Located just beyond the old city, the flea market is an essential Jaffa experience. Best approached from Olei Zion Street, where it meets Jerusalem Boulevard, this sprawling warren of streets is lined with shops that sell everything from very expensive refurbished antique and art deco furniture to junk from someone's grandmother's attic. The whole place buzzes with energy and oozes local charm. Shopkeepers who have known one another for years shout greet-

ings, or sit around sipping mint tea and playing backgammon. Bargaining is possible in some places, to a limited extent. But unless you grew up in a Turkish bazaar, don't expect to pull one over on these seasoned merchants – they are far too street smart for the average shopper.

There are several cafes, tiny pubs and restaurants tucked in between the shops in the flea market. All are charming places to stop for a meal or a snack, but if there is one eatery that is a "must," it's Dr. Shakshuka. This legendary, no-frills restaurant serves home-style traditional cuisine originating with the Jewish communities in Tripoli and Morocco. It is most famous, however, for its signature dish: shakshuka, or eggs cooked in a spicy tomato sauce, which is practically a national delicacy. Served in the frying pan, this richly satisfying meal is scooped up with chunks of fresh bread and washed down with mint tea or lemonade.

The **American Colony**

Just behind the flea market and Jerusalem Boulevard, in a sort of no-man's land that links Florentin to Jaffa, lies the American Colony. This tiny, picturesque neighborhood of wooden homes with gabled roofs looks as though it was transported from a New England museum about life in the nineteenth century – which it was, in a way.

In 1866, a group of American Evangelical Christians from Jonesport, Maine docked in Jaffa, bringing with them the wood they used to build their homes in the holy land. They later sold the tiny colony to German Templars, which is why it is sometimes referred to as the German Colony. The story of the American Colony is told at the Maine Friendship House, which is open daily to visitors.

Jerusalem Blvd.

Crowded and often noisy with traffic, Jerusalem Boulevard is one of Jaffa's main shopping arteries and thoroughfares. It throbs with lively activity throughout the week. The shops run the gamut from local bakeries to fashionable design emporiums, so there is a lot of pedestrian traffic, making this an interesting place to stroll and people watch.

The internationally acclaimed Gesher Theater, which frequently produces plays with English surtitles and is definitely worth a visit, dominates the northern end of Jerusalem Boulevard. Behind the fountain square is the charming Noga Quarter, where several design studios, fashionable shops, cafes and restaurants are located between beautifully restored Ottoman-era residential buildings.

Yefet St.

Built at the beginning of the twentieth century to celebrate the silver anniversary of Sultan Abd al-Hamid II, the three-story clock tower is Jaffa's most famous landmark. Today it dominates the plaza that marks the beginning of Yefet Street, just at the point where Tel Aviv merges into Jaffa. The side streets in this area are a bit gritty (also known as "authentic") and crowded, but well worth exploring. They are lined with casual restaurants that are patronized by local characters, many of whom while away their afternoons over endless games of cards and backgammon, played at rickety tables set up on the sidewalks.

Just a little further up Yefet Street one comes to Abulafia, which is easily the most famous bakery in the city. It is open 24 hours a day, and there is nearly always a crowd of customers gathered around. Piping hot pita bread rolls off the conveyer belt and the shelves are piled with sweet and savory Levantine pastries.

Along with Jerusalem Boulevard, Yefet is one of Jaffa's two most important commercial streets. Besides its cafes, shops and restaurants, it is famous for its landmarks – like St. Anthony's Church, or Fakhri Geday's pharmacy, which has been in the same location and under the same family's ownership since the British mandate period.

Stop in at Yafa Café at 33 Yehuda Margoza Street, where it meets Yefet. Co-owned by a Jewish woman and an Arab man, this intimate, book-lined café is a well-known local hangout for journalists and academics. For dessert, try the Victory ice cream shop next door – it's a local institution.

Deeper into **Jaffa**

Tourists do not tend to explore much past the attractions of the old port, the flea market and a few fish restaurants. The only real exception to the rule is Ali Karavan, popularly known as Abu Hassan's, which is widely considered the best hummus joint in Israel. Given that Israelis are completely obsessed with hummus, this is saying a great deal. If you want to check out this 40-year-old legendary hole-in-the wall, it's just down the hill on Dolphin Street. But get there early – by mid-afternoon the hummus is usually all gone, and on Fridays a queue of people starts to gather from early in the morning for their weekend treat.

Jaffa is filled with charming side streets, picturesque courtyards and lush gardens that are great fun to explore. The restored Ottoman homes in the old port are inhabited mostly by the rich, but Ajami and the rest of Jaffa are where the regular people live. This is really the only place in greater Tel Aviv where Jews and Arabs live side-by-side. Many point to Ajami as a particularly good example of peaceful co-existence.

The darker side of Jaffa is its reputation for criminal activity – mostly drug related. There are frequent turf wars between rival gangs that sometimes manifest themselves in shooting incidents. There has never been a case of an innocent bystander being caught in the crossfire, so the local media rarely reports these incidents. Jaffa is also known for petty crime – mostly car and house break-ins. But none of this should frighten visitors away. The streets are perfectly quiet and safe – particularly during the day – and in any case Israel is almost completely free of the type of violence that is so prevalent in major Western cities.

There are several beautiful, landmark old homes in Ajami, especially around the areas of Yefet, Toulouse and Kedem Streets. The signs of gentrification are unmistakable, as is the evidence of poverty, but overall this is a laid-back, authentic neighborhood with a friendly atmosphere. Take your time walking around here – there are lots of interesting things to discover.

Café Paul, at 142 Yefet, is a cozy neighborhood hangout where rich espresso made from beans roasted on the premises is served to appreciative regular customers. The ice cream parlor next door has been around for years, and is immensely popular. The row of shops that includes Café Paul is right around the corner from the French ambassador's residence, appropriately located on Toulouse Street. This impressive Bauhaus landmark was originally commissioned as a private residence for a prominent Arab family. The Arab-Jewish community center and elementary school lie just ahead, around the open space that serves as a local park. The historic Muslim and Greek Orthodox cemeteries that overlook Ajami beach are also a fascinating place to visit.

Take a right on Kedem and walk along the beach; there are some good, inexpensive seafood restaurants that are patronized by locals. There are also several nargileh bars, where local men (and sometimes women) hang out to smoke, play backgammon and drink mint tea. The local mosque is a simple affair – the call to prayer is chanted by a real live person with a pleasantly modulated voice, rather than played from a scratchy recording via a public address system.

In a way, Jaffa and Tel Aviv feel like two different countries. Together, though, they create a unique fusion of Levantine, Arab, European, Jewish, modern and ancient influences that characterize the unique city of Tel Aviv-Jaffa.

Food

[Map 1]

Cordelia

1 Simtat Hazchuchit, corner of 30 Yefet St.
Tel. (03) 518 4668
www.cordelia.co.il

Named for the loyal youngest daughter of King Lear, Cordelia is indeed a restaurant worthy of a princess. Candles and crystal chandeliers illuminate this renovated Crusader building, highlighting the wine goblets, mosaic tile floors, antique paintings, and dark wooden tables. The romantic atmosphere enfolds diners as they experience some of the most imaginative cuisine in Israel. Celebrity Chef Nir Zook never fails to evoke smiles of pleasure – particularly with his famous seven-dish degustation menu. Updated each month, the degustation is inspired by classic French cuisine and local, seasonal ingredients. The result is an unforgettable fusion of French and Mediterranean flavors that consistently garners praise from food critics - and renewed vows of loyalty from Cordelia's many regular patrons.

Food

Noa Bistro

14 Hatzorfim St.
Tel. (03) 518 4668
www.cordelia.co.il

Several years after Cordelia rose to fame, Chef Nir Zook opened Noa Bistro in the inner courtyard of the same ancient Crusader complex. The eclectic décor features plants and strings of dried red peppers hanging from the high ceilings, vases of fresh flowers and enormous armchairs grouped around low tables to create corners for intimate conversation. The overall impression is one of sophistication and elegance. The food is every bit as striking as the décor. The chef creates classic bistro dishes with his trademark innovative interpretations, at surprisingly comfortable prices. With his three-course business lunch, Nir Zook proves that the price of a gourmet meal need not be prohibitive, even if it is accompanied by a glass of excellent wine.

[Map 2]

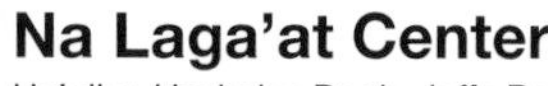

Theater & Food

Na Laga'at Center

Ha'aliya Hashniya Dock, Jaffa Port
Tel. (03) 633 0808
www.nalagaat.org.il

[Map 3]

Is it possible for the deaf-blind to communicate their inner world to those who can see and hear? If so, what does it feel like to live in a world of silence and darkness? What kind of hopes and emotions do the deaf-blind experience? Na Laga'at ("Do Touch") is a theater group of deaf-blind actors who answer these questions in their extraordinarily powerful, touching and richly humorous performances of original plays that are based on their own lives. Narrated in Hebrew, the plays are accompanied by sign language interpretation and surtitles in English and Arabic. This unforgettable theater experience succeeds in touching the audience at a deeply primordial level, earning rave reviews for sold-out performances even in jaded New York.
The architecturally distinguished Na Laga'at Center includes a café and a gourmet restaurant. At Café Kapish deaf waiters, who communicate using easily understood sign language, serve upscale café food in airy, attractive surroundings. Celebrity Chef Nir Zook is the culinary advisor to the extraordinary Blackout Restaurant, where kosher meals are served in pitch darkness by blind wait staff.

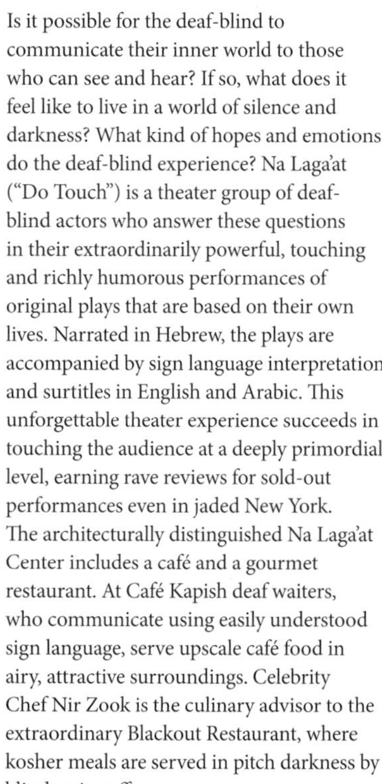

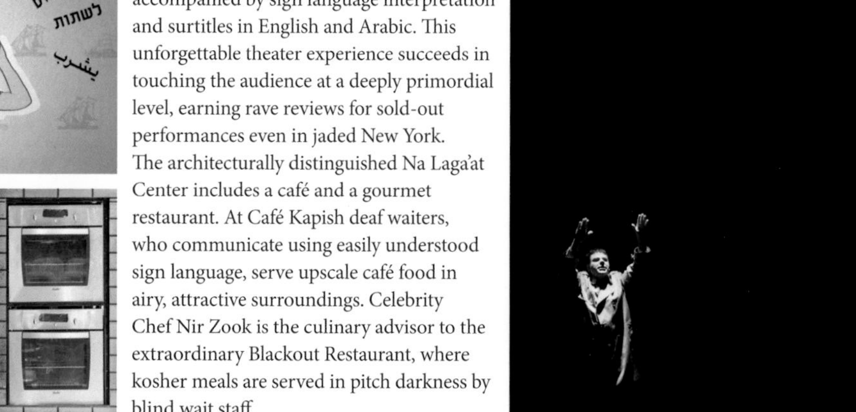

)esign

Riva

0 Nechama St., Noga Area
el. (077) 781 3542
(050) 781 3542
www.designbyriva.com

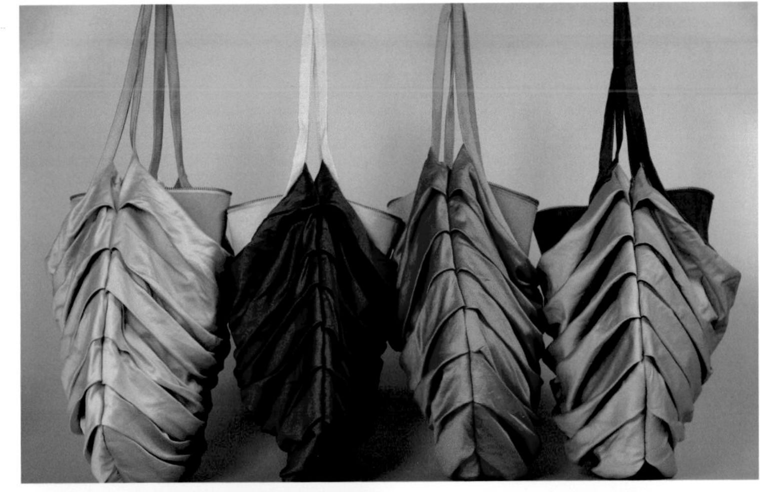

Having established her reputation as designer of innovative, quality bags for upscale stores through Israel, Riva Jaroshevitch recently opened her own studio boutique in Jaffa's Noga Square. Here she creates and sells her collections of day and evening bags in leather, copelle and fabrics, as well as a line of instantly appealing wallets and belts. Riva's intelligent, classic designs combine color, sophistication and aesthetics to striking effect. The attention to detail is expressed both in the workmanship and the designs, which range from colorful fabric daypacks to unique accessories.

[Map 4]

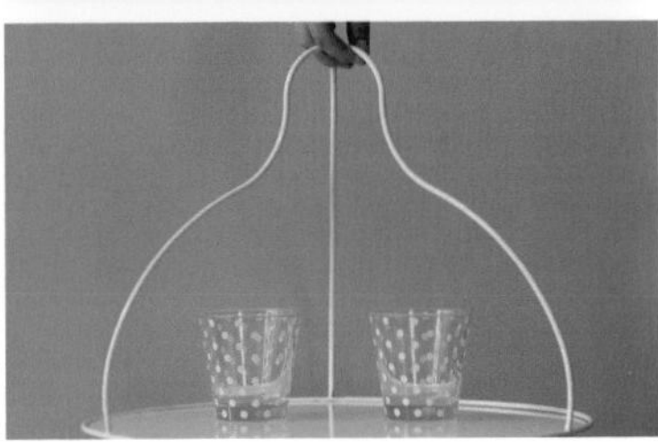

Design

Extra Vergine

1 Hapninim St.
Tel. (03) 682 2905
www.extravergine-design.com

[Map 5]

Tucked away in an ancient Jaffa alley, just steps from the sea, Extra Vergine design studio and atelier is suffused with Mediterranean light and style. This is where designers Viola and Ram Bar-Zeev create their beautiful lampshades, trays and other decorative accessories, combining local influence and universal principles of modern design for a strikingly attractive effect. Archetypal Levantine coffee and tea trays are re-imagined using modern prints and bold colors, while the lampshades carry evocative names like "Arabesque" and " Provence."

Public Space

Jaffa Port

Old Jaffa Port
Tel. (03) 683 2255
www.namalyafo.co.il

[Map 6]

Nearly every afternoon, fishermen sit on the dock at Jaffa Port, repairing their nets while their boats bob gently in the waters of the marina. This is a classic Levantine port scene, but Jaffa is special. Steeped in 4,000 years of history, it is the oldest working port in the world.

Over the past few decades the port was badly neglected, with warehouses falling into ruin and visible crumbling of the dock. The Tel Aviv-Jaffa municipality has now undertaken a multi-phase renewal project that will simultaneously repair the damage and bring cultural and commercial value to the port, while preserving its traditional character and purpose.

The first phase of this project, which will be completed by the fall of 2009, calls for the renovation of the architecturally distinguished 1930s warehouse facing the marina. Once a packing warehouse for Jaffa oranges, the renovated 5,500 square meter building will contain a variety of businesses, galleries and performance spaces, combining culture and commerce under one roof .

Soon, a pedestrian bridge will connect the dock to the wave breaker, allowing strollers to view the walls of the ancient city of Jaffa from the water, just as tourists, invaders, pilgrims and merchants saw it when they approached the city by ship, hundreds of years ago.

More of the Best

Food

Ali Karavan

1 Hadolphin St., Old Jaffa

Popularly called "Abu Hassan," after the late owner, this glorious hole in the wall is a national hummus icon. The daily batch is all gone by 2 p.m., so make sure to arrive early - and don't be surprised if you're asked to share a table.

Design

4 Make

32 Yefet St.
Tel. (03) 518 3213
www.4make.com

A design studio for unique pictures and decorative photographs.

Hotel

Andromeda

3 Louis Pasteur St.
Tel. (03) 683 8448

Beautiful holiday rental apartments in restored Old Jaffa, just steps from the best restaurants and cafés in the area.

Café, Gallery

Horace

34 Olei Zion St.
Tel. (077) 216 0041

Delicious, creative cafe fare is served on locally made ceramic dishes at Horace, which is located at the edge of the flea market. The stylishly restored Ottoman interior is filled with light and decorated with gorgeous, unusual ceramics imported from Uzbekistan. The objects for sale in the gallery section include whimsical jewelry and elaborate vases.

Food

House No. 3

3 Amiad St.
Tel. (03) 681 4052
www.housethree.co.il

Located just across from the flea market, this stunningly restored and decorated Ottoman-era home belongs to Leila and Hamoudi Habashi. Hamoudi is a former fisherman turned French-trained chef, while Leila is a designer and perfect hostess. Together they host unforgettable pre-fixe dinners for small groups that must reserve well in advance.

Night

Jaffa Bar

30 Yefet St.
Tel. (03) 518 4668
www.cordelia.co.il

Just a step away from Cordelia, this cozy ba oozes nostalgia and charm. Chef Nir Zook oversees the wonderful a la carte meals here, too.

Food

Poyke, African Steaks & Bar

14 Tirza St., Noga area
Tel. (03) 681 4622

Chef Ariel Cohen traveled around southern Africa to learn how to cook meat in a poyke a traditional African cast iron cooking pot. He brought his knowledge back to Tel Aviv, added his own culinary ingenuity and created a unique new fusion food concept that combines beef, seafood and unusual African spices.

Café

Pua

8 Rabbi Yochanan St., Flea Market
Tel. (03) 682 3821

Located in the middle of the flea market, Pua is one of the best-known cafés in Jaffa. It's a lovely place to sit, enjoy a meal, linger over a coffee and soak up the local atmosphere.

Night

Saloona

17 Tirza St., Noga area
Tel. (03) 518 1719

Located in a beautifully renovated old Ottoman-era building, Saloona is one of the most stylish lounge bars in the city. The DJ's are excellent, the crowd is young, beautiful and hip, and there are changing ar exhibitions to view as well.

Design

Workshop

15 Yefet St.
Tel. (03) 518 5928

Father-daughter design team Zvi and Hadas Shaham create eye-catching, eclectic furniture, lamps, accessories and jewelry that show both contemporary and retro influences.

Food

Yoezer Wine Bar

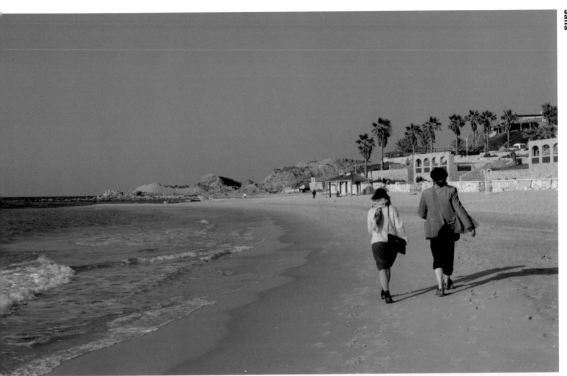

2 Yoezer Ish Habira St.
Tel. (03) 683 9115

Located in an impressive Ottoman era building, Yoezer Wine Bar is a cozy, grotto-like space where diners enjoy the chef's acclaimed gourmet French-country cuisine, along with the widest selection of international vintages available in Israel.

Design

Uma

3 Ben Yair St.
Tel. (03) 682 2290

African and tribal decorative objects are sold in this huge, high-ceilinged gallery shop.

100 Centennial Celebrations

From April-December 2009, Tel Aviv-Jaffa will celebrate the city's centennial with a series of cultural, historical and interactive events– ranging from a performance of Verdi's Aida by La Scala, to a citywide marathon. The following is a list of events that will appeal to international visitors.

February 2009

Electronic Music and Video–Art Festival

February 10-23: Tel Aviv – Jaffa will host an innovative electronic music and video art festival, featuring leading local and international artists. The event will showcase a variety of electronic genres, ranging from orchestral arrangements to club music.

April 2009

Gala Opening

April 4: International artists, the Israel Opera and the Israeli Philharmonic, led by Maestro Zubin Mehta, will give a gala performance at Rabin Square, while an audiovisual display is projected on the buildings around the square.

International Conference on Urban Innovation

April 1-2 2009: Tel Aviv – Jaffa's population is 400,000, and it continues to grow annually. As the centennial year events begin, the city will host experts, journalists, and international guests from its 24 sister cities to discuss the most up-to-date issues dealing with the urban sphere of the twenty-first century.

Spirit of the Century Project

April 1-4 2009: A kite-flying event will fill the sky with color, while thousands of mobiles built by children and their families will hang from windows and balconies throughout the city. Meanwhile, children will sail paper boats with greetings for the city along the Yarkon River.

Tel Aviv Marathon

April 17th: The plan is to make the Tel Aviv Marathon into an annual tradition, attracting participants from all over the world. Shorter courses, of 5 and 10 kilometers, will be offered in addition to the traditional 42-kilometer run.

May 2009

Tel Aviv-Jaffa on the Silver Screen

The Tel Aviv Cinematheque celebrates its 25th anniversary this year. To celebrate the city and the Cinematheque there will be a series of tributes and events. These include screenings of films made in or about Tel Aviv, an international film festival, a short film contest, special student film competitions and a special event focusing on the Eden Cinema in Neve Tzedek, which was Israel's first movie theater.

Les Ballets de Monte Carlo

The renowned ballet troupe will perform in Tel Aviv's Performing Arts Center.

June 2009

Inauguration of the Bialik Compound

A new museum reflecting the history of Tel Aviv-Jaffa will be inaugurated in the original city hall on Bialik Street, with a multi-disciplinary exhibition of 100 years of Tel Aviv art. The nearby Reuven Rubin Museum will mount an exhibition of works by famous Tel Aviv artists.

White Night

Each year, for one night in the month of June, the city of Tel Aviv stays up until dawn to enjoy free museum admission, live performances of music, theater and dance on the streets and boulevards, installation art and many, many more events. This year the White Night will be particularly festive, with special events related to Tel Aviv's centennial in the Bialik Compound.

Castles in the Sand Exhibition

The Eretz Israel Museum will feature an exhibition of photographs, memories and legends of the Tel Aviv-Jaffa shoreline.

July-August 2009

Culture Park

During the summer of 2009, Ganei Yehoshua will become the Israel Culture Park. Hundreds of thousands of visitors from all over the country are expected to come for the concerts, which range from Carmen performed by the Israel Opera to live Hasidic music; Batsheva, Israel's world-renowned modern dance troupe, will perform Anaphaza; and there will be many other music performances representing an eclectic and fascinating range of genres. There will also be photography and art exhibitions.

La Scala

In July 2009 La Scala will perform in Israel for the first time. Franco Zeffirelli will conduct Verdi's Aida at the Tel Aviv Performing Arts Center, followed by a one-time performance of Verdi's Requiem at the Caesarea Ampitheater.

Tel Aviv-Jaffa's Secret History

Antiques and archaeological artifacts found around Tel Aviv will be exhibited at the Eretz Israel Museum in August.

The 18th Maccabiah Games

The 18th Maccabiah Games will pay tribute to the first Hebrew city, as the birthplace of this major sporting event. Many of the games will take place in Tel Aviv, which will also host a massive beach party for the 10,000 participating athletes and coaches from all over the world.

Tributes to Tel Aviv-Jaffa's sister cities

New York, Paris, Moscow, Beijing, Buenos Aires, Barcelona, Frankfurt, Milan and Budapest are all connected to Tel Aviv with various Sister City and Friendship agreements. Throughout the summer, each city will participate in events at various venues around the city, during which the sister cities pay tribute to one another.

September 2009

Carpet Flower

The month of the Jewish High Holy Days will be marked this year with several unique events: to greet the Jewish New Year, a giant carpet of flowers will be unfurled to reveal a secret message; many Jewish delegations from the Diaspora will celebrate the holy days in Tel Aviv-Jaffa; and there will a communal Sabbath-greeting ceremony, composed of both secular and religious Jews, at the Tel Aviv port.

October 2009

October is Green Month. To celebrate ecological awareness within the context of the centennial, the municipality will hold an ecological festival in cooperation with the Society for the Protection of Nature in Israel. At the same time, 100 kilometers of bicycle paths will be paved and marked throughout the city.

The International Harp Contest

Celebrating its 50th anniversary in 2009, the International Harp Contest draws visitors and music fans from all over the world. Many of the contest's winners have gone on to stellar careers as harpists in leading orchestras.

Loving Art

Each fall, Tel Aviv's galleries and art museums launch new exhibitions of works by exciting local artists. This year, the artistic offering will be even wider.

November-December 2009

The final two months of the centennial celebrations include several historical and cultural events.

The Founders Conference

The descendants of the city's founders will gather to speak about the future of Tel Aviv-Jaffa. In a multi-generational tribute, portraits of the founders will be exhibited next to photographs of the youngest generation of descendants.

Open House Tour

Residents of Tel Aviv's heritage homes will open their doors to guided tours for one day.

Alexander Calder Retrospective

The Tel Aviv Museum of Modern Art will show works by the renowned American sculpture artist in an exhibition that will be a sort of artistic theme park.

International Business Conference

Tel Aviv is one of the world's most important centers worldwide for high-tech, venture capital, international banking and diamond trading. As such, it attracts a great deal of interest from foreign investors. The international business conference will capitalize on Tel Aviv's existing reputation while promoting business ventures and economic development. Foreign investors and international companies from all over the world will participate.

Closing Event

A final closing event will be a festive culmination of the centennial events.

A full list of events can be found on the Centennial Website,
at **www.tlv100.co.il**

For more information:

Tel Aviv-Jaffa Centennial Administration

1 Zeitlin Street, 3rd Floor,
Tel Aviv, 64956

Tel. (03) 725 3861
Fax. (03) 695 9684
E. tlv100@mail.tel-aviv.gov.il

www.tlv100.co.il

Cultural Tel Aviv

Museums

Ben Gurion House
17 Ben Gurion Blvd
Tel. (03) 522 1010

Bialik House
22 Bialik St.
Tel. (03) 525 4530

Center for Contemporary Art
5 Kalisher St.
Tel. (03) 510 6111
www.cca.org.il

Diaspora Museum
Tel Aviv University Campus
Tel. (03) 745 7800

Eretz Israel Museum
2 Haim Levanon St.
Tel. (03) 641 5244
www.eretzmuseum.org.il

Haganah Museum
23 Rothschild Blvd.
Tel. (03) 560 8624

Hapalmach Museum
10 Haim Levanon St.
Tel. (03) 643 6393

Helena Rubinstein Pavilion
6 Tarsat St.
Tel. (03) 528 7196
www.tamuseum.com

Ilana Goor Museum
4 Mazal Dagim St., Old Jaffa
Tel. (03) 683 7676
www.ilanagoor.com

Independence Hall
16 Rothschild Blvd.
Tel. (03) 517 3942

Israel Army Museum
35 Eilat St.
Tel. (03) 516 1346

Jabotinsky Institute
38 King George St.
Tel. (03) 621 0611

Nachum Gutman Museum
21 Rokach St., Neve Tzedek
Tel. (03) 516 1970
www.gutmanmuseum.co.il

Rokach House
36 Rokach St., Neve Tzedek
Tel. (03) 516 8042

Rubin Museum
14 Bialik St.
Tel. (03) 525 5961
www.rubinmuseum.org.il

The Bible House
16 Rothschild Blvd.
Tel. (03) 517 7760

Tel Aviv/Zaritsky Artist's House
9 Alharizi St.
Tel. (03) 524 6685

The Genia Schreiber Gallery at the Tel Aviv University
Gate 7, Tel Aviv University, Ramat Aviv
Tel. (03) 640 9022

The Tel Aviv Museum of Art
27 Shaul Hamelech Blvd.
Tel. (03) 607 7000
www.tamuseum.com

Galleries

AAI - Art Agency Israel
Show Room - by appointment only
8 Achva St.
Tel. (03) 516 3186
www.artagency.co.il

Alfred Gallery
13 Florentin St.
Tel. (054) 541 2213

Alon Segev Gallery
23 Shaul Hamelech Blvd.
Tel. (03) 609 0769
www.alonsegevgallery.com

Art Space // Kunsthalle for Contemporary Art
69 Rothschild Blvd.
www.artspace.co.il

Artist's Studio
18 Elifelet St.
Tel. (03) 683 0505

Bineth Gallery
15 Frishman St.
Tel. (03) 523 8910
www.binethgallery.com

Braverman Gallery/ By Art Project
12B Hasharon St.
Tel. (03) 566 6162
www.byartprojects.com

Chelouche Gallery for Contemporary Art
5 Hissin St.
Tel. (03) 528 9713
www.chelouchegallery.com

D&A Gallery
57 Yehuda Halevi
Tel. (077) 450 8010
www.gallerydanda.com

DAP Dollinger Art Project
18 Frishman St.
Tel. (03) 527 6994
www.dollingerartproject.com

Dvir Gallery
11 Nachum St.
Tel. (03) 604 3003
www.dvirgallery.com

Farkash Gallery
5 Mazal Dagim St.
Tel. (03) 683 4741
www.farkash-gallery.com

Florentine 45
45 Florentin St.
Tel. (050) 276 3249

Gallery 39 for Contemporary Art
39 Nachmani St.
Tel. (03) 566 6631
www.artgallery39.com

Gallery Harel, Printers & Publishers
8 Elizabeth Bergner St.
Tel. (03) 681 6834
www.harelart.com

Gal-On Gallery
79-81 Yehuda Halevi St.
Tel. (03) 560 3222

Gilit Fisher Gallery
9 Bezalel Yafe St.
Tel. (077) 400 6358

Givon Art Gallery
35 Gordon St.
Tel. (03) 522 5427
www.givonartgallery.com

Gordon Gallery
95 Ben Yehuda St.
Tel. (03) 524 0323
www.gordongallery.co.il

Hakibbutz Gallery
25 Dov Hoz St.
Tel. (03) 523 2533
www.kibbutzgallery.org.il

Hamidrasha Art Gallery
34 Dizengoff St.
Tel. (03) 620 3129

Heder Art Gallery
11 Gottlieb St.
Tel. (03) 522 2402
www.theheder.com

Inga
2 Harakevet St.
Tel. (03) 560 0812

Julie M
10 Bezalel Yafe St.
Tel. (03) 560 7008
www.juliem.com

Kav 16
6 Sheshet Hayamim St.
Neveh Eliezer Community Center
Tel. (03) 730 0360

Nelly Aman
26 Gordon St.
Tel. (03) 523 2003

Noga Gallery of Contemporary Art
60 Ahad Ha'am St.
Tel. (03) 566 0123
www.nogagallery.co.il

Peer
42 Mazeh St.
Tel. (03) 528 2299

Raw Art
3 Shvil Hameretz St., Building 8
Tel. (03) 683 2559
www.rawartint.com

Rosenfeld
147 Dizengoff St.
Tel. (03) 522 9044
www.rg.co.il

Solo Gallery
7 Solomon St., Old Central Bus Station
Tel. (03) 636 5720

Sommer Contemporary Art
13 Rothschild Blvd.
Tel. (03) 516 6400
www.sommergallery.com

Stern
30 Gordon St.
Tel. (03) 524 6303
www.sternart.com

Tavi Dresdner
24 Ahva St., Neve Tzedek
Tel. (077) 787 0605
www.tavidresdner.com

Cultural Centers

Beit Lessin Theater
101 Dizengoff St.
Tel. (03) 725 5333
www.lessin.co.il

Beit Ariela Cultural Center
25 Shaul Hamelech Blvd.
Tel. (03) 691 0141

Habima -The National Theater
2 Tarsat Blvd.
Tel. (03) 526 6666
www.habima.co.il
(The National Theater is currently under construction, and will reopen in 2009.)

Hasimta Theater
8 Mazal Dagim St., Jaffa
Tel. (03) 681 2126

Heichal Hatarbut (Culture Center)
1 Huberman St.
Tel. 1 700 703 030
www.hatarbut.co.il

Gesher Theater
9 Jerusalem Blvd.
Tel. (03) 681 3131
www.gesher-theatre.co.il

Suzanne Dellal Center for Dance & Theater
5 Yechieli St.
Tel. (03) 510 5656

The Cameri Theater
19 Shaul Hamelech Blvd.
Tel. (03) 606 0960
www.cameri.co.il

The Israel Philharmonic Orchestra
Mann Auditorium
1 Huberman St.
(03) 629 0193
www.ipo.co.il

The Israel Opera Tel Aviv-Yafo
19 Shaul Hamelech Blvd.
Tel. (03) 692 7777
www.israel-opera.co.il

Tmuna Theater
8 Shonchino St.
Tel. (03) 562 9462

Tzavta
30 Ibn Gvirol St.
Tel. (03) 695 0156

ZOA, Zionist Organization of America House
26 Ibn Gvirol St.
Tel. (03) 695 9341

Music Venues

Barby
52 Kibbutz Galuyot St.
Tel. (03) 518 8123
www.barby.co.il

Barzilay Club
13 Harechev St.
Tel. (03) 687 8090
www.barzilayclub.com

Club 24
3 Hata'arucha St.
Tel. (03) 602 1542
www.music24.co.il

Cultura
154 Herzl St.
Tel. (03) 518 7238

Levontin 7
7 Levontin St.
Tel. (03) 560 5084
www.myspace.com/levontine7

Zappa
24 Raul Wallenberg St., Ramat Hachayal
Tel. (03) 767 4646
www.zappa-club.co.il

The Felicja Blumental Music Center
26 Bialik St.
Tel. (03) 620 1185
www.fbmc.co.il

Shablul Jazz Club
Hangar 13, Tel Aviv Port
Tel. (03) 546 1891
www.shabluljazz.com

Movie Theatres

Tel Aviv Cinematheque
2 Sprinzak St.
Tel. (03) 606 0800

Dizengoff Cinema
Dizengoff Center
Tel. (03) 620 3303

Gat
62 Ibn Gvirol St.
Tel. *2202

Globus
Azrieli Shopping Mall
Tel. (03) 608 1131

Lev Dizengoff
Dizengoff Center
Tel. (03) 621 2222

Rav Chen Dizengoff
Dizengoff Square
Tel. (03) 528 2288

Rav Chen Opera
1 Allenby St., Opera Tower
Tel. (03) 510 2674

Useful Numbers

Tel Aviv-Jaffa City Hall
69 Ibn Gvirol St.
Tel. 1 599 588 888
www.tel-aviv.gov.il

Tourist information Center
46 Herbert Samuel St., corner of 2 Geula St., Tel Aviv Promenade
Tel. (03) 516 6188
Hours: Sunday to Thursday: 09:30-17:30, Friday: 09:30-13:00

Police
100

Medical emergency/ Ambulance
101

Fire Department
102

Post Office

170 Ibn Gvirol St.
Tel. (03) 604 1109
www.postil.com

61 Hayarkon St.
Tel. (03) 510 0218
www.postil.com

61 Herzl St.
Tel. (03) 682 5856
www.postil.com

Hospitals

The Tel Aviv Sourasky Medical Center (Ichilov Hospital)
6 Weizmann St.
Tel. (03) 697 4444
www.tasmc.org.il

Assuta Hospital
62 Jabotinsky St.
Tel. (03) 520 1507
www.assuta.co.il

Pharmacies

London MiniStore SuperPharm
4 Shaul Hamelech Blvd.
Tel. (03) 696 0115

Allenby Street SuperPharm
115 Allenby St.
Tel. (03) 510 4111

Gordon Street SuperPharm
129 Dizengoff St., corner of Gordon St.
Tel. (03) 529 9566

Taxis

Balfour Taxis
59 Balfour St.
Tel. (03) 560 4545

Habima Taxis
4 Tarsat Blvd.
Tel. (03) 538 3131

Hayarkon Taxis
101 Hayarkon St.
Tel. (03) 522 3233

Hatzfon Taxis
20 Yermiyahu St.
Tel. (03) 602 0210

Nordau Taxis
16 Nordau Blvd.
Tel. (03) 546 6222

Road service

Shagrir
Tel. (03) 557 8888
www.shagrir.co.il

Europe Assistance
Tel. (03) 953 5600

Transportation

Egged Bus Company
Tel. (03) 694 8888
www.egged.co.il

Dan Bus Company
Tel. (03) 639 4444
www.dan.co.il

Israel Airports Authority
www.iaa.gov.il

Ben Gurion Airport
Tel. (03) 975 5555 - Information
(03) 972 3333 - Arrivals & Departures
www.iaa.gov.il

Israel Railways
Tel. (03) 611 7000
www.israrail.org.il

Credit Card

American Express
Tel. (03) 636 4292

MasterCard
Tel. (03) 636 4400

Visa
Tel. (03) 572 6666

Free walking tours of Tel Aviv-Jaffa with English-speaking guides

The following tours are given year round, and require no advance booking.

Bauhaus – The White City

Every Saturday, at 11:00 a.m.
Meeting point: 46 Rothschild Blvd., corner of Shadal St.

The White City tour focuses on the examples of Bauhaus-influenced architecture on Rothschild Boulevard. This tour is a wonderful opportunity to savor the experience of Tel Aviv life, past and present.

www.white-city.co.il

Tel Aviv **by Night**

Every Tuesday at 8 p.m.

Meet on Rothschild Boulevard at Herzl Street for a nighttime historical tour of Tel Aviv, narrated with stories and anecdotes that connect the events of the past to the contemporary atmosphere.

Tel Aviv University: **Art and Architecture**

Every Monday at 11:00 a.m.
Meeting point: Dyonon bookstore: campus entrance at Haim Levanon and Einstein Streets.

A tour of Tel Aviv University's campus architecture.

Old **Jaffa**

Every Wednesday at 9:30 a.m.
Meeting point: Clock Tower, Yefet Street, Jaffa.

The tour covers the flea market, archeological sites, the view of Tel Aviv and the restored alleys of Old Jaffa.

Index

Cafés

Food

Jos & Los *139*
51 Yehuda Halevi St.
Tel. (03) 560 6385

Kimmel *174*
6 Hasha'ar St.
Tel. (03) 510 5204

Kyoto *140*
31 Montefiore St.
Tel. (03) 566 1234

Lilit *96*
2 Dafna St.
Tel. (03) 609 1331

Manta Ray *170*
Alma Beach, near the Etzel Museum
Tel. (03) 517 4773
www.mantaray.co.il

Meat Bar *96*
52 Chen Blvd.
Tel. (03) 695 6276

Messa *80*
19 Haarba'a St.
Tel. (03) 685 6859
www.messa.co.il

Mezze *140*
51a Ahad Ha'am St.
Tel. (03) 629 9753

Moon *96*
58 Bograshov St.
Tel. (03) 629 1155

Mul Yam *55*
Hangar 24, Tel Aviv port
Tel. (03) 546 9920

NG *174*
6 Ahad Ha'am St.
Tel. (03) 516 7888

Nana Bar *174*
1 Ahad Ha'am St.
Tel. (03) 516 1915

Noa Bistro *191*
14 Hatzorfim St.
Tel. (03) 518 4668
www.cordelia.co.il

Onami *96*
18 Haarba'a St.
Tel. (03) 562 1172

Orna and Ella *135*
33 Sheinkin St.
Tel. (03) 620 4753

Pasta Mia *140*
10 Wilson St.
Tel. (03) 561 0189

Pastis *140*
73 Rothschild Blvd.
Tel. (03) 525 0773

Poyke, African Steaks & Bar *196*
14 Tirza St., Jaffa
Tel. (03) 681 4622

Pronto *119*
26 Nachmani St.
Tel. (03) 566 0915
www.pronto.co.il

Radio Rosco *140*
97 Allenby St.
Tel. (03) 560 0334

Raphael *97*
87 Hayarkon St.
Tel. (03) 522 6464

Sakura *97*
79 King George St.
Tel. (03) 621 2900

Shila *55*
182 Ben Yehuda St.
Tel. (03) 522 1224

Shibuya *97*
28 Bograshov St.
Tel. (03) 620 4927

Stefan Braun *140*
99 Allenby St.
Tel. (03) 560 4725

Sushi Samba TLV *49*
27 Habarzel St., Ramat Hachayal
Tel. (03) 644 4345
www.sushisamba.com

Suzanna *172*
9 Shabazi St.
Tel. (03) 517 7580

Tahel *175*
30 Nachalat Binyamin St.
Tel. (03) 516 8410

Tapeo *97*
16 Haarba'a St.
Tel. (03) 624 0484

Thai House *97*
8 Bograshov St.
Tel. (03) 517 8568

Toto *87*
4 Berkovich St.
Tel. (03) 693 5151

Vince & Tamar *140*
10 Hatzfira St.
Tel. (03) 639 0407

Yoezer Wine Bar *197*
2 Yoezer Ish Habira St., Jaffa
Tel. (03) 683 9115

Zepra *97*
96 Yigal Alon St.
Tel. (03) 624 0044

Night

Abraxas *173*
40 Lilienblum St.
Tel. (03) 510 4435

Academia *138*
6 Montefiore St.

Armadillo *138*
51 Ahad Ha'am St.
Tel. (03) 620 5573

Armadillo Cerveza *95*
174 Dizengoff St.
Tel. (03) 529 3277

Artemis *173*
52 Nachalat Binyamin St.
Tel. (03) 510 0663

Atara *138*
32 Rothschild Blvd.

Averbuch *95*
2 Reines St.
Tel. (03) 523 7719

Bar Barbunia *53*
192 Ben Yehuda St.
Tel. (03) 524 0961

Barzilay *138*
13 Harechev St.
Tel. (03) 687 8090

Brasserie M&R *70*
70 Ibn Gvirol St.
Tel. (03) 696 7111

Breakfast Club *138*
6 Rothschild Blvd.

Bugsy *173*
26 Florentin St.
Tel. (03) 681 3138

Bukovsky *95*
39 Frishman St.
Tel. (03) 523 2323

Clara *173*
1 Koifman St., Dolphinarium area
Tel. (03) 510 2060

Eliezer *43*
186 Ben Yehuda St.
Tel. (03) 527 5961

Erlich *54*
3 Hata'arucha St., Tel Aviv port
Tel. (03) 546 6728

Evita *139*
31 Yavneh St.
Tel. (03) 566 9559

Gilda *139*
64 Ahad Ha'am St.
Tel. (03) 560 3588

Hamara *96*
87 Hayarkon St.
Tel. (03) 522 6464

Ha'oman 17 *174*
88 Abarbanel St.
Tel. (03) 681 3636

Jaffa Bar *196*
30 Yefet St.
Tel. (03) 518 4668

Jajo *174*
47 Shabazi St.
Tel. (03) 516 4557

Jewish Princess *139*
67 Yehuda Halevi St.
Tel. (03) 560 2223

La La Land *96*
Gordon Beach
Tel. (03) 529 3303

Lenny's *174*
7 Vital St.
Tel. (03) 518 6637

Levontin 7 *140*
7 Levontin St.
Tel. (03) 560 5084

Lima Lima *174*
42 Lilienblum St.
Tel. (03) 560 0924

Mental *130*
7 Shadal St.
Tel. (03) 560 5655

Messa *80*
19 Haarba'a St.
Tel. (03) 685 6859
www.messa.co.il

Mishmish *174*
17 Lilienblum St.
Tel. (03) 516 8178

Minerva *174*
98 Allenby St.
Tel. (03) 560 5595

Molly Bloom's *96*
2 Mendele St.
Tel. (03) 522 1558

Nanuchka *174*
28 Lilienblum St.
Tel. (03) 516 2254

Rosa Parks *55*
256 Dizengoff St.

Saloona *196*
17 Tirza St. (Noga area)
Tel. (03) 518 1719

Satchmo *175*
6 Vital St.

Shalvata *38*
3 Hata'arucha St., Tel Aviv port
Tel. (03) 544 1279

Shesek *175*
17 Lilienblum St.
Tel. (03) 516 9520

Silon *97*
89 King George St.
Tel. (03) 620 0053

Toma *97*
26 Ibn Gvirol St., ZOA House
Tel. (03) 695 6804

Whisky a Go Go *39*
3 Hata'arucha St., Tel Aviv port
Tel. (03) 544 0633
(054) 560 2262

Ice Cream

Amoretto *95*
21 Ibn Gvirol St.
Tel. (03) 525 0602

Bacho *95*
85 King George St.
Tel. (03) 528 9753

Iceberg *96*
108 Ben Yehuda St.
Tel. (03) 522 5025

Iceberg Vulcano *54*
Fountain Square, Tel Aviv port
Tel. (03) 602 6000

Savta Ice Cream *175*
9 Yechieli St.
Tel. (03) 510 5545

Tartufo *175*
25 Shabazi St.
Tel. (03) 517 0505

Tel Hanan Ice Cream *97*
68 King George St.

Vanilia *55*
22 Ashtori Hafarchi St.
Tel. (03) 602 0185

Design

Arbitman's *82*
31 Gordon St.
Tel. (03) 527 8254

Arik Ben Simhon *173*
110 Nachalat Binyamin St.
Tel. (03) 683 7865

Armani Casa *53*
3 Hata'arucha St.
Tel. (03) 544 3306

BaBoo *166*
34 Yedidia Frenkel St.
Tel. (03) 682 8885
www.be-baboo.com

Bauhaus Center Tel Aviv *78*
99 Dizengoff St.
Tel. (03) 522 0249
www.bauhaus-center.com

Blue Bandana *34*
52 Hei Beiyar St.
Tel. (03) 602 1686

Carousella *139*
27 Rothschild Blvd.
Tel. (03) 560 3750

Elemento *139*
119 Rothschild Blvd.
Tel. (03) 620 9848

Eretz Israel Museum Shop *50*
Eretz Israel Museum, Tel Aviv
2 Haim Levanon St., Ramat Aviv
Tel. (03) 641 5244 (ext. 8)
www.eretzmuseum.org.il

Extra Vergine *193*
1 Hapninim St.,Jaffa
Tel. (03) 682 2905
www.extravergine-design.com

Habitat *90*
2 Ibn Gvirol St.
71 Ibn Gvirol St.
43 Carlebach St.
Tel. (03) 695 1282
www.habitat.co.il

Hadarim *174*
48 Salame St.
Tel. (03) 681 0678

Hafatzim *174*
27 Chelouche St.
Tel. (03) 517 8744

Kastiel & Sons Design Center *156*
36 Alfasi St.
Tel. (03) 683 6334

Nook *89*
5 Malchei Israel St.
Tel. (03) 527 7177
www.nook.co.il

Retro-TLV *129*
123 Yehuda Halevi St.
Tel. (03) 685 0663
www.retro-tlv.com

Rugine *140*
46 Montefiore St.

Salon Saloma *97*
25 Gordon St.
Tel. (03) 527 4150

Samy D. *162*
56 Shabazi St.
Tel. (03) 516 4968
www.samy-d.com

Sarit Shani Hay *126*
36 Nachmani St.
Tel. (03) 566 6987
www.shanihay.com

Serendipity Lifestyle Gallery *175*
30 Chelouche St.
Tel. (03) 516 6045

Tali's Lifestyle Design *159*
8 Ahad Ha'am St.
Tel. (03) 510 8848

Tollman's *73*
71 Ibn Gvirol St.
Gan Ha'ir shopping complex
Tel. (03) 522 3236
www.tollmans.co.il

Uma *196*
3 Ben Yair St.,Jaffa
Tel. (03) 682 2290

Villa Maroc *118*
110 Yehuda Halevi St.
Tel. (03) 562 0401
www.villamaroc.co.il

Workshop *196*
15 Yefet St.
Tel. (03) 518 5928

4 Make *196*
32 Yefet St.,Jaffa
Tel. (03) 518 3213
www.4make.com

Fashion

Alma *138*
9 Merkaz Ba'alei Melacha St.
Tel. (03) 620 0145

Anny & Adi Jacobson *53*
224 Ben Yehuda St.
Tel. (03) 544 2444

Art-C-Ifrach *115*
5 Barzilay St.
Tel. (077) 553 3455
www.art-c-ifrach.com

Babette *173*
31 Shabazi St.
Tel. (03) 510 0534

Banker *53*
210 Dizengoff St.
Tel. (03) 529 0358

Banot - Loulou Liam *36*
212 Dizengoff St.
Tel. (03) 529 1175
www.loulouliam.com

Closet Collection *134*
12 Harekevet St.
Tel. (03) 560 2571

comme il faut house at the port *42*
Hangar 26, Tel Aviv port
Tel. (03) 602 5530
www.comme-il-faut.com

Delicatessen *139*
4 Barzilai St.
Tel. (03) 560 2297

Dina Glass *139*
35 Nachmani St.
Tel. (03) 560 2493

FabLab Fabiani *35*
280 Dizengoff St.
Tel. (03) 602 5569
www.fablabfabiani.com

Frau Blau *139*
8 Hachashmal St.
Tel. (03) 560 1735

Frida *47*
190 Dizengoff St.
Tel. (03) 522 5151
www.frida.co.il

Gertrud *54*
225 Dizengoff St.
Tel. (03) 546 7747

Gusta *51*
19 Jabotinsky St.
Tel. (077) 323 0038
www.myspace.com/gustastore

Ido Recanati *96*
13 Malchei Israel St.
Tel. (03) 529 8481

Katomenta *96*
173 Dizengoff St.
Tel. (03) 527 9899
www.katomenta.com

Mayu Rabin Square *77*
7 Malchei Israel St.
Tel. (03) 527 3992

Mayu Neve Tzedek *158*
15 Shabazi St.
Tel. (03) 516 6975

Mizo *174*
51 Shabazi St.
Tel. (03) 516 4105

Motherland *54*
38 Basel St.
Tel. (03) 546 0611

Nona Elga *125*
12 Barzilay St.
Tel. (03) 560 1257

Oberson Fashion House *89*
36 Gordon St.
Tel. (03) 524 3822
www.oberson.co.il

Ronen Chen *97*
155 Dizengoff St.
Tel. (03) 527 5672

Sarah Braun *78*
162 Dizengoff St.
Tel. (03) 529 9902

Sharon Brunsher *121*
12 Harekevet St.
Tel. (03) 560 4834
www.brunsher.com

Shine *140*
12 Harakevet St.
Tel. (03) 560 1658

Tanti Becky *83*
63 Bar Kochva St.
Tel. (03) 525 5995

Tovale *55*
220 Dizengoff St.
Tel. (03) 524 9929

Tovale's *55*
220 Dizengoff St.
Tel. (03) 529 8987

Yosef *55*
213 Dizengoff St.
Tel. (03) 529 8991

Bags, Shoes and Accessories

Behonot *138*
11 Sheinkin St.
Tel. (03) 620 9295

Couple Of *53*
207 Dizengoff St.
Tel. (03) 529 1098

Daniella Lehavi *46*
34 Basel St.
Tel. (03) 544 0573
www.daniellalehavi.com

FabLab Fabiani *35*
280 Dizengoff St.
Tel. (03) 602 5569
www.fablabfabiani.com

Gaya *43*
5 Alkalay St.
Tel. (03) 602 2747
www.gayashoe.co.il

Kisim *140*
8 Hachashmal St.
Tel. (03) 560 4890

More Design *125*
12 Harekevet St.
Tel. (03) 560 5297

Precious *97*
63 Frishman St.
Tel. (03) 529 3814

va 193
Nechama St., Noga Area, Jaffa
(077) 781 3542
(050) 781 3542
w.designbyriva.com

ufra 97
3 Dizengoff St.
(03) 524 7274

140
Harakevet St.
. (03) 560 1482

ewelry

gas and Tamar 167
3 Shabazi St.
l. (03) 516 8421
ww.agasandtamar.com

yala Bar 173
6 Shabazi St.
l. (03) 510 0082

ori Csengeri 48
42 Dizengoff St.
l. (03) 604 3273
ww.doricsengeri.com

. Stern 54
ilton Tel Aviv Hotel
l. (03) 524 9619

iller 96
57 Dizengoff St.
l. (03) 524 9383

rit Ivshin 169
3 Shabazi St.
l. (03) 516 0811
ww.oritivshin.com

adani 55
6 Hei Beiyar St.
el. (03) 695 1254

aula Bianco 135
2 Harekevet St.
el. (03) 685 0171
www.paulabianco.biz

uby Star 124
28 Levontin St.
el. (077) 560 6500
www.rubystar-accessories.com

hai Lahover 55
203 Dizengoff St.
el. (03) 523 3887

ael Herman Gallery 52
11 Dizengoff St.
l. (03) 522 1816
(052) 367 6647
ww.yaelherman.com

ooks and Music

ookworm 95
Malchei Israel St.
el. (03) 529 8490
ww.bookworm.co.il

mily 95
9 Ben Gurion Blvd.
el. (03) 523 9624

Khotam Books 139
55 Sheinkin St.
Tel. (03) 685 2350

Librairie Du Foyer 83
14 Masaryk Square
Tel. (03) 524 3835
www.librairie.co.il

Pollak 97
36 King George St.
Tel. (03) 528 8613

Sipur Pashut 168
36 Shabazi St.
Tel: (03) 510 7040
www.sipurpashut.net

Steimatzky 97
109 Dizengoff St.
Tel. (03) 522 1513
www.steimatzky.co.il

Sketchbook 129
5 Tchernichovsky St.
(03) 620 1351
www.sketchbook.co.il

The Third Ear 97
48 King George St.
Tel. (03) 621 5200

Tzomet Sfarim / Proza 97
163 Dizengoff St.
Tel. (03) 523 5477
www.booknetshop.co.il

Yoga and Pilates

Bikram Yoga 95
14 Carlebach St.
Tel. (03) 624 1807

Ella Yoga 53
Hangar 4, Tel Aviv port
Tel. (03) 544 4881

Dror Raz Pilates 174
5 Yechieli St.
Suzanne Dellal Center
Tel. (03) 510 8527

Iyengar Yoga Center 174
2 Chelouche St.
Tel. (03) 516 3641

Pilates by Dalia Mantver 55
62 Hei Beiyar St.
Tel. (03) 544 5344

Yoga at Gan Hachashmal 120
9 Levontin St.
Tel. (03) 560 1225
www.goyoga.co.il

Beauty

Collie Hair Design 128
141 Rothschild Blvd.
Tel. (03) 685 2020
www.collie.co.il

Luck 40
5 Alkalay St.
Tel. (03) 544 2252
www.luckworld.co.il

Miki Buganim 54
1 Pinkas St.
Tel. (03) 546 3242

Eyewear

Claude Samuel 79
17 Dizengoff St.
Tel. (03) 620 8882

Food & accessories boutiques

4 Chef 140
11 Carlebach St.
Tel. (03) 561 1803

Brill Cigars 53
194 Dizengoff St.
Tel. (03) 527 0707

Devidas 53
1 Yehuda Hamaccabi St.
Tel. (03) 602 1602

Hinawi 96
25 Carlebach St.
Tel. (03) 624 0458

Olia 75
73 Frishman St.
Tel. (03) 522 3235
www.olia.co.il

Hotels

Andromeda 196
3 Louis Pasteur St., Jaffa
Tel. (03) 683 8448

Art + Hotel 92
35 Ben Yehuda St.
Tel. (03) 542 5555
www.atlas.co.il

Center Hotel 92
2 Zamenhoff St.
Tel. (03) 526 6100
www.atlas.co.il

Cinema Hotel 93
1 Zamenhoff St.
Tel. (03) 520 7100
www.atlas.co.il

Dan Tel Aviv 95
99 Hayarkon St.
Tel. (03) 520 2525
www.danhotels.com

David Intercontinental 173
12 Koifman St.
Tel. (03) 795 1111
www.InterContinental.com

Hilton Tel Aviv 54
Independence Garden
Tel. (03) 520 2222
www.hilton.com

Hotel Montefiore 116
36 Montefiore St.
Tel. (03) 564 6100
www.hotelmontefiore.co.il

Melody Hotel 44
220 Hayarkon St.
Tel. (03) 521 5300
www.atlas.co.il

Nina Suites Hotel 164
29 Shabazi St.
Tel. (052) 508 4141
www.ninacafehotel.com

Prima Tel Aviv 76
105 Hayarkon St.
Tel. (03) 520 6666
www.prima.co.il

Sea Executive Suites 132
76 Herbert Samuel St.
Tel. (03) 795 3434
www.sea-hotel.co.il

Sheraton Tel Aviv Hotel & Towers 86
115 Hayarkon St.
Tel. (03) 521 1111
www.sheraton.com/telaviv